WEIRD AND WACKY

Places and things to do that you'll hardly believe

Sally and Gordon Hammond

NEW
HOLLAND

First published in Australia in 2005 by
New Holland Publishers (Australia) Pty Ltd
Sydney • Auckland • London • Cape Town

14 Aquatic Drive Frenchs Forest NSW 2086 Australia
218 Lake Road Northcote Auckland New Zealand
86 Edgware Road London W2 2EA United Kingdom
80 McKenzie Street Cape Town 8001 South Africa

Hammond, Sally .
Weird & wacky places.
ISBN 1 74110 180 8.

1. Travel - Miscellanea. 2. Curiosities and wonders. I.
Title.

910.2

Publisher: Fiona Schultz
Project Editor: Jacqueline Blanchard
Editor: Glenda Downing
Designer: Karl Roper
Production Controller: Kellie Matterson
Printer: Times Offset, Malaysia

10 9 8 7 6 5 4 3 2 1

DISCLAIMER
While many places and events
have been highlighted in this book,
readers are advised and expected
to follow their own judgment. They
should pay particular attention to
national and international alerts
and travel advisories current at the
time they plan to travel, especially
regarding the safety and security
of travelling to, or participation in,
any countries, places or activities
mentioned in this book. The
publisher and authors take no
responsibility for any death, injury
or loss occasioned by any of the
people, destinations or activities
featured in this book.

PREFACE

Travel has never been easier, yet it can become such a serious business, and in all the rush and bustle of connecting flights and crammed schedules sometimes it's possible to forget to have fun. So we thought, why not celebrate the marvellously zany, wacky and downright weird things in this world, as well as the strange and sometimes crazy things on the world's calendar? The entries in this book are all true and correct, according to our research, with contact details included so you can go and check them out for yourself.

Do so, and we guarantee you'll travel with a smile on your face. May your journeys be seasoned with weird and wonderful experiences.

And if you find something fascinating in your travels that you would like to share—contact the publishers. Who knows? We may need to put together another volume. After all, it is a weird and wacky world! Join us now, in celebrating this unique place in which we live.

— Sally and Gordon Hammond

ACKNOWLEDGMENTS

Obviously books like this don't just happen. We are indebted to the many people who loved the idea of a weird little book like this and fed us ideas and sent pictures. Also to the team at New Holland for making this book happen.

DIG THIS PLACE

Ever wished you could beat the heat? Try getting down and dirty. Well, down anyway.

The 150 or so locals of White Cliffs, a tiny outback opal-mining town 255 kilometres north-east of Broken Hill, have got the idea. They burrow their homes deep underground where the temperature stays at an ambient 22°C all year, night and day—a cool escape from the above-ground temperature which might hit 40°C.

Plenty of people visit the place each year to try their luck searching for opals, and so the Underground Motel was dug out—an extension of the original owner's home. The place 'just grew' until there were 32 rooms, shared bathrooms ('off-suite' they call them), a licensed restaurant, bar and gift shop. The rooms are bright and clean with whitewashed earth walls—but no windows, of course.

Guests spend their days opal fossicking and with a bit of luck pay off their holiday with what they find. Lucky or not, the opal bug bites hard, and many return year after year to try their chances.

The Underground Motel & Restaurant

White Cliffs NSW 2836
AUSTRALIA
Phone: +618 8091 6677
info@undergroundmotel.com.au
www.undergroundmotel.com.au

DEEP SLEEP

Take your PJs to PJ's, but be prepared to disappear into your burrow to put them on.

Certainly a B&B with a difference, PJ's Underground is dug out under the baking hot earth—the owners call it their 64 million-year-old roof—in the small town of White Cliffs, hundreds of kilometres west of Sydney.

Australia's first commercial opal fields are here, and originally all that the tired miners wanted to do at the end of the day was to escape the extreme heat. So they carved out their homes underground, some right beside their opal diggings, and found a constant temperature to revive them.

Even though you're metres underground, don't expect to get dirty at PJ's. The walls are whitewashed, the five guest rooms are comfy, and there is even a spa. You can pretend you're a real pioneer here (or even a Hobbit if you wish), play prospector, then feast on home-grown vegetables (from PJ's ground-level garden) and homemade bread.

PJ's Underground

Dugout 72, Turley's Hill
White Cliffs NSW 2836
AUSTRALIA
Phone: +618 8091 6626;
pjsunderground@bigpond.com
http://babs.com.au/pj

DOWN UNDER DOWNUNDER

Coober Pedy, 846 kilometres north of Adelaide, is almost an upside-down town. It's hot here in the centre of Australia, so even the Serbian Orthodox Church—still with delicate religious art and stained glass—is located underground.

The Desert Cave Hotel is the centrepiece of this opal-mining town that supplies about 40 per cent of the world's opals. Billed as the world's only underground hotel, it offers international-standard dining and accommodation, underground shops and opal display areas, a bar and convention facilities.

While there are above-ground rooms, the underground ones feature walls that look as if they have been just carved out of the rock, with brown worm-like marks that are part of the sandstone here. Visitors say that sleeping underground gives them the best night's sleep they have ever had.

Come at Easter for Coober Pedy's Opal Festival, or at other times you can just 'noodle' around, looking for scraps of opal around the edges of the diggings. Who knows, you could get very lucky and pick up a really valuable souvenir.

Desert Cave Hotel
PO Box 223
Coober Pedy SA 5723
AUSTRALIA
Phone: +618 8672 5688
reserve@desertcave.com.au
www.desertcave.com.au

MAD HIDEAWAY

Actually you'd be mad *not* to try the Hatters Hideout, where you can make like a troglodyte and hide away in a cave with candles and an open fire.

A stay in Hat Cave is intended as an environmental retreat for family and small groups, 'like renting a private national park'. That's because the views over the Wollemi wilderness are unrivalled.

This area has another claim to the bizarre. A 40-metre prehistoric pine tree, belonging to a species believed to have been extinct for 60 million years, was discovered in Wollemi Forest. Who knows what else is lurking out there? There have been sightings of a prowling black panther in recent years, so anything is possible. Whatever! You'll be safe in your cave, which has been sculpted by nature—a huge sandstone cathedral with a 25-metre-high arched opening and 30-metre-tall rock columns or 'pagodas'.

Hatters Hideout

Blue Mountains NSW
AUSTRALIA
Phone/fax: +612 6355 2777
hatter@hattershideout.com.au
www.hattershideout.com.au

Weird and Wacky · 13

EN-CHANTING

Nan Tien is the largest Buddhist temple in the southern hemisphere, and this imposing structure includes an eight-storey pagoda, containing three shrines and about 10 000 buddhas.

What's more, in the museum you'll find an engraved strand of human hair—yes, really—on which someone, using a sharpened grain of rice, has inscribed 28 words. This amazing act is attributed to an elderly Taiwanese Buddhist, who was obviously a very patient, keen-sighted person.

Many visitors come for a visit by day, but some people choose to stay on at the Pilgrim Lodge. There are weekend and short-term meditation retreats year-round at the temple, and meals are available.

The sounds of a gong and drum awaken guests each morning and mark the end of the day in the evening, but you do not have to be a Buddhist to come and stay here. Although you may certainly learn more from the lessons on Buddhism, many people come simply to reflect and meditate, or attend vegetarian cooking or Tai Chi classes. Some stay to research the symbolism and architecture of this very beautiful temple.

Nan Tien Temple

Berkeley Rd (PO Box 1336)
Unanderra NSW 2526
AUSTRALIA
Phone: +612 4272 0500
nantien@ozemail.com.au
http://members.ozemail.com.au/~nantien

LAVA-LY

Lava tunnels, over-friendly kookaburras, and a train that goes nowhere. What a wacky combination. Yet this seems to be what people want as Undara Lava Lodge was voted winner in the Unique Accommodation category of the Australian Tourism Awards in 2003.

First there's the lava. Undara Volcanic National Park is 275 kilometres southwest of Cairns in northern Queensland. The Undara lava tubes are believed to be the largest and longest on the planet and so-named because the local Aboriginal word for 'long way' is—you guessed it—Undara.

Around 190 000 years ago, a volcano erupted here spilling molten lava into dry riverbeds. As the outside cooled it formed pipelines for the fiery lava, then hardened to leave dark, hollow tubes, ideal now for exploring.

Tired and hungry explorers need somewhere to crash for the night though. So 23 ex Queensland Government Rail sleeper carriages dating back to 1888 have been hauled in and fitted out for dining and accommodation. And the kookaburras? Watch out! If you're not careful these brash birds will steal the meat from your plate as you dine on the outdoor deck under the gum trees.

Undara Lava Lodge

ndara Volcanic Park
Savannah Way, Undara Qld
AUSTRALIA
(Undara Experience, PO Box 6268, Cairns Qld 4870)
Phone: +617 4097 1411, Freecall 1800 990 992 (Aust);
info@undara-experience.com.au   res@undara.com.au
www.undara.com.au

CRIKEY!

Most people treat crocodiles with caution, and few would be silly enough to attempt to curl up with one for the night. But central Australia's Gagudju Crocodile Holiday Inn expects its guests to do just this. But that's not as dangerous as it sounds—this place is built in the shape of a crocodile.

The hotel is 250 metres from head to tail and 30 metres across the belly. Guests enter through the croc's jaws, but the marble foyer is less threatening. It's designed to represent a cool, green billabong.

The crocodile is of great cultural significance to the Gagudju, the local Aboriginal people, and this hotel was designed in consultation with them.

Really out the back of the Back of Beyond, Gagudju is approximately 2.5 hours' drive from Darwin along the Arnhem Highway in the remote Kakadu National Park in the Northern Territory.

The hotel restaurants serve plenty of local Australian and indigenous foods, including barramundi, buffalo and kangaroo—and appropriately you may even tuck into crocodile at times there too.

Gagudju Crocodile Holiday Inn

Flinders Street
Jabiru NT 0886
AUSTRALIA
Phone: +618 8979 9000
hotel@crocodileholidayinn.com.au
http://gagudju-crocodile.holiday-inn.com

PLATYPUS PARADISE

Here is some trivia. What is a monotreme? It's an egg-laying mammal, and Australia has the only two examples of them: an echidna and a platypus.

Wazza, Scruffy and Roada are the hosts at this so-Australian place, established fifteen years ago, where you can sleep up a tree, shower in the rainforest and, hopefully, catch a glimpse of one of the shyest animals in the world.

There are three timber slab tree-huts, a bush kitchen for making damper and billy tea, and a place to sit by the campfire and dream.

You can play at being in the Garden of Eden in this pristine environment. Apart from platypus there are hosts of birds, as well as frogs, reptiles, and marsupials—those pouched little furry critters. At night, fruit bats silently pass between the trees and fireflies light up the darkness.

But don't stay up too late. Platypus are best seen early in the morning, in the creek that bubbles along beside the camp.

Platypus Bush Camp

Gorge Road (PO Box 29)
Finch Hatton Gorge Qld 4756.
AUSTRALIA
Phone: +617 49583204
wazza@bushcamp.net
www.bpf.com.au/platypus_bush_camp.htm

DO A BUNK

The Visitors' Bunk Room at the Grove Creek Observatory is just that. It's not meant to be five-star accommodation. At night, anyway. Located at the rear of the observatory, the bunk room is more a place to un-crick your neck after a few hours of star-gazing.

Everyone talks about the stars in the outback. The fact is, here you can see a hundred times more than in the city, as there is no glow from streetlights, cars and houses. The nearest habitation, the tiny town of Trunkey, with a population of just 50 people, is six kilometres away.

The observatory—the first built in this part of NSW in 1985—is regarded as one of the best dark sky locations in the southern hemisphere at 972 metres altitude with a 360° clear horizon. Which, if you are into astronomy, will make you want to head there fast.

No need to take a pillow, though. The bunk room is fully set up for when you finally do need to get the stars out of your eyes.

The Grove Creek Observatory
Trunkey NSW 2741
AUSTRALIA
Phone: Sydney office: +612 9438 1516 (2pm–9pm AEST only)
Observatory phone: +612 6368 8611 (2pm–7pm AEST only)
info@gco.org.au
www.gco.org.au

PLAYING POSSUM

Not many people know that the Brisbane Line was developed during World War II as a line of defence against a possible Japanese invasion of Australia. Extensive underground concrete bunkers were constructed and equipped at this site near Miles, over 200 kilometres west of Brisbane.

After the war the bunkers fell into disuse—well, how often do you have need of a spare bunker, after all? It was not until 1985, when David and Julie Hinds bought the property, that the possibilities were realised.

They set about refurbishing eight of the original 20 bunkers to turn them into cool and comfortable underground accommodation, adding wartime railway carriages as self-contained cabins. Some of the larger underground bunkers were turned into a morning tea room, souvenir shop and rest facilities.

There's plenty of memorabilia on display as well, but it is still hard to imagine that these bunkers once held 2500 tonnes of bombs and ammunition—enough to make quite a dent in any advancing army.

The feared invasion never came. The explosives have been removed, and all that remains is a tribute to another era—and a unique place to stay.

Possum Park
Bunker 18
Miles Qld 4415
AUSTRALIA
Phone/fax: +617 4627 1651
enquiries@murilla.qld.gov.au
www.murilla.qld.gov.au/visitors/possum.shtml

DIS-LODGE

Sail past this elegant wilderness lodge any time between May and October and your only thought will be 'how can I get to stay there myself?' Come back between November and April and you will blink twice as this vision of luxury will have disappeared.

This floating lodge is positioned in the shelter of Barnard Harbour on Princess Royal Island, British Columbia. Each Spring it dislodges from its warm-weather mooring to be towed to Prince Rupert in Autumn.

But King Pacific Lodge is no steel and chrome cruise ship. It looks just like a three-storey lodge—a very comfortable one with gables and balconies and verandas, finished with fir timber, natural slate and wrought-iron. Inside, there's custom-made furniture and every luxury for around 25 very privileged people.

So why come here? Guests enjoy fly-fishing, kayaking, spa treatments, or simply soaking up the sun and gazing at the water and forests as the occasional seal or whale cruises past and eagles fly overhead. What a life!

King Pacific Lodge

Suite 214, 255 West 1st Street
North Vancouver BC V7M 3G8
CANADA
Phone: +160 4987 5452
or toll-free 888 592 5464
info@kingpacificlodge.com
www.kingpacificlodge.com

STAY IN JAIL—DO NOT PASS GO

Fancy a stretch in jail? Maybe a night is all you can stand—particularly if it's at the site of Canada's last public hanging.

Patrick Whelan was the condemned man, guilty of the murder of Thomas D'Arcy McGee, one of the fathers of the Confederation. But his was just one of a long line of deaths in this grim place.

The HI-Ottawa Jail Hostel is a Hostelling International property open year-round and priced affordably—with lower rates for members, of course. There is private accommodation, although not in a cell, and there are dormitory beds as well. You may visit death row and the gallows during a historical jail tour, and hear stories that will turn you pale.

As you would expect for a jail, the building is centrally located, and is an easy walk to all of the city's major attractions.

And as you may have also guessed—it is also said to be one of Canada's most haunted buildings.

Sleep well!

HI-Ottawa Jail Hostel

75 Nicholas Street
Ottawa Ontario K1N 7B9
CANADA
Phone: +1 613 235-2595
www.hihostels.ca/hostels/Ontario/OntarioEast/OttawaInternationalHostel/Hostels/index.html

CHILL OUT!

Most people like to snuggle up and keep warm at night, and surprisingly you can do this at the Ice Hotel Quebec on deer hide covers. Even though the walls, floor, ceiling—yes, even the beds—are made from over 12 000 tonnes of snow!

Following the trend of very cold places overseas, Quebec decided that it should have an ice hotel too, the only one in North America. There is even an ice chapel for the coolest wedding imaginable. But, unlike other hotels in the world, this one not only gets a regular refurbishment but it is *built* each year from the purest building material on the planet.

Obviously, you need to pick your booking times carefully, this Cinderella hotel is open for just months each year, from early January to early April. With sparkling walls over a metre thick, the air inside stays at a constant $-2°C$ to $-5°C$, often warmer than outside in a Quebec winter. Oh, and in case you are wondering, the bathrooms are heated.

Ice Hotel Quebec

143 route Duchesnay, Pavillon l'Aigle
Sainte-Catherine-de-la-Jacques-Cartier
Quebec G0A 3M0
CANADA
Phone: +141 8875 4522
toll-free Can/USA: 877 505 0423
marketing @icehotel-canada.com
www.icehotel-canada.com

SNOW WAY TO LIVE

Travel way north to Rovaniemi right on the Arctic Circle and find the line of latitude plainly marked for you to cross—and of course photograph yourself doing so as well. Then, experience the Lapp(land) of luxury, book into a specially built igloo, the Luminna—Snowland, sit on a snow bench (thoughtfully covered with reindeer skin) and enjoy a hot meal.

But this is about the only warmth in this very unusual hotel, open each year from January to March, depending on the weather. A maximum of twenty people can be accommodated here in four-person igloos with insulated snow-beds. Breakfast is served by the fire in a nearby kota, the Lapp version of a tepee.

Of course guests dress warmly to come here, but the hotel also provides special gear, and the tables and seats in the dining room have been insulated so everything—the meal and you—keep warm for the duration.

Lumimaa—Snowland

Kiviniementie, Rovaniemi 5 96400
LAPLAND
Phone: +358 16 316 500
lapland@fintravel.com
www.snowland.fi/snowland.html

TREE-MENDOUS

An island hideaway, sand dunes, tamarind trees and a Buddhist ecological theme park filled with temples, gardens and pagodas next door. What more could you want? Try adding a tree house for accommodation, accessible only by a swaying suspension bridge.

The Big Beach in the Sky Tree House, one of the four tree houses on the site, sleeps six comfortably in two levels and a loft. From there it is just as long as it takes to reach the beach, before you are splashing in the South China Sea. There is even a Spa Tree House built amongst the branches of another tamarind tree.

Across the ocean, in a forest by a lake, the same owners run the Hawaiian Hale Hotel Tree House that accommodates sixteen to twenty guests in seven separate spaces on three levels. Others prefer the Beach Club Tree House above the Hawaiian Beach Club.

Whatever the choice, you can expect all guests here have a 'high' time.

Sanya Nanshan Treehouse Resort and Beach Club

Sanya Nanshan, Hainan
CHINA
Phone: +86 138 0750 0909
chinatreehouses@yahoo.com
www.treehousesofhawaii.com/nanshan.html

CROCO-NILE

Take the kids to the temple of Kom Ombo, between Luxor and Aswan in Upper Egypt, and watch their eyes pop. The Mummified Crocodile room in this Indiana Jones-type setting complete with perfectly preserved crocs jutting out from the walls, will stay in their memories forever.

Getting there is just as memorable—via a felucca cruise on the longest river in the world—although the oldest-ever felucca, the 5000-year-old Solar Boat in the museum next to the Pyramids is a bit of an eye-opener too. Its journey was meant to have been even longer and stranger: on sunbeams between Orion and Earth. Feluccas, or Egyptian yachts, have sailed the Nile since ancient times. Royal feluccas once carried the image of the pharaoh, and Napoleon even had his own one to explore Upper Egypt.

Today the MS *Cleopatra*, a lateen-rigged 62–foot Nile sailing vessel, has sleeping accommodation for two to six people and adds a private Egyptologist to answer any questions if needed. So, it seems, while you may not be able to 'walk like an Egyptian', at least you can say that you have sailed like one!

Royal Cleopatra—Felucca Travel

Post St # 506
San Francisco CA 94109 USA
Phone: +141 5440 1124
info@nubiannilecruises.com
omar@travelinstyle.com
www.nubiannilecruises.com/
egypt/royalcleo/royalcleo7days.html

STATION-ARY

If the *Orient Express* is out of your budget, there is an answer. At the former Petworth Railway Station, built in 1894, you can board a carriage and at least pretend you're off to Venice. Built around the time of the *Titanic,* these British Pullman carriages have survived much longer, and have now been beautifully restored into four very grand suites, although like any old-timer, each has its own personality and many stories to tell.

Guests breakfast either on the platform, in the original booking hall (with a roaring log fire in winter) or in their carriage, and romantic champagne breakfasts are available by request.

Even the former waiting room has a touch of class with its six-metre vaulted ceiling. The station master's office is now the station kitchen, but still retains the original ticket windows.

It's the golden-age of rail all over again. The *Orient Express* without a hint of Agatha Christie. Way to go! Or not to go, depending on how you look at it.

The Old Railway Station

Petworth West Sussex GU28 0JF
ENGLAND
Phone: +44 1798 342 346
query@old-station.co.uk
www.old-station.co.uk

DUST OFF YOUR TIARA

If you've always hankered after being royal, or even if you just want to have an above-stairs experience for once, this could be the answer.

The 24 hectares of gracious riverside gardens are open year round, and the Hampton Court Palace shows off 500 years of royal history, including the state apartments of Henry VIII and William III to tourists from all over the world. There's even a world-famous maze.

But of most interest to us common folk is that there are two Landmark Trust apartments in the 18th-century manse at Hampton Court which may be let for holidays. Just make sure you book well ahead if you want to be one up on your friends.

It is unlikely that you will be bothered by the ghost of Lady Catherine Howard, Henry VIII's fifth wife, who is said to stroll the corridors, and you will be able to have a little out-of-tourist-hours enjoyment of the gardens. And while you won't have a valet or a lady-in-waiting at your disposal, you will be able to drop phrases into the odd dinner party conversation later, such as, 'You know, when I stayed at Hampton Court Palace …'

Hampton Court Palace

East Molesey Surrey KT8 9AU
ENGLAND
Phone: Information line: +44 870 752 7777
www.landmarktrust.org

SLEEP LIKE THE DEAD

At least the neighbours won't disturb you at this—oh, so quiet place.

The Chapel of Rest is a sandstone Victorian gothic chapel is dead centre among the graves, with a heavy lancet door, and cast-iron lattice on the stained glass windows. It's Derbyshire's smallest B&B, but if it seems a bit gothic to book into a graveyard for your holiday, think of it this way. You are surrounded by generations of formerly upright (now horizontal) citizens of this small village. The Chapel has been resurrected with cosy furnishings, a bathroom, and an antique wooden bed.

So how do you follow a night in a graveyard? Try moving to the other building, run by the same owners. The Old Lock Up is where DH Lawrence and wife Frieda, a German citizen listed as an alien in World War I, reported weekly to the authorities. Now it too has a new life, with the original heavily barred door one of the few remaining reminders.

Chapel of Rest, Old Lock Up

North End Wirksworth Derbyshire DE4 4FG
ENGLAND
Phone/fax: +44 1629 826272
wheeler@theoldlockup.co.uk
www.theold lockup.co.uk

SNOW SHOWS

The Snow Restaurant and Mammut Snow Hotel opened on the Gulf of Bothnia, Finland at the beginning of 2004, and will give guests a chilly welcome from January to mid-April each year. Way too cool for school, the university students from nearby Rovaniemi on the Arctic Circle, have decorated the hotel rooms in textiles designed to reflect the Arctic environment. While the temperature in the rooms is around −5°C, this is still the wimp's way to experience an Arctic winter, where the outside temperature might plummet to −25°C or more.

Guests stay toasty warm, though, in Ajungilak sleeping bags designed for extreme climate zones and expeditions, and supplied by sister snow-country, Norway. In the ice-sculpture decorated restaurant, guests dine at ice tables while seated on reindeer fur that covers (surprise!) ice seats. Want more? The adjoining Snow Castle opens daily for a light and sound showing of icy artwork.

Oy LumiLinna Kemi

SnowCastle Ltd
Kemi
Lapland, FINLAND
Phone: +358 16 259 502
www.snowcastle.net

BECOME A CAVE-PERSON

Perivolas is a complex of 17th-century private 'houses', yet they are quite plainly different from most. The fact is, locals lived like this for centuries, and this group of 300-year-old caves were once a village of fishermen's and farmer's houses plus their outbuildings.

Today, the caves are classier, but the whitewashed domed ceilings are a giveaway that these places are actually built into the hillside. They also have superb views over the Aegean. So on the Greek ilsand of Santorini you have caves that ended up as a hotel complex with front desk services, massage sessions and motorbike rentals.

The island itself is worth exploring too. Earthquakes and volcanoes have tried to shake the land, and it is said that the lost city of Atlantis is buried in the island's caldera. The only thing that hasn't changed over all these many years is the spectacle of Oia's dramatic sunsets.

Perivolas Traditional Houses

GR 847 02 Oia Santorini
GREECE
Phone: +30 2867 1308
info@perivolas.gr
www.perivolas.gr

LOVE MATCH

Just staying in a four-star (Europe's highest hotel rating) hotel on an island in the Seine should be fascinating enough, but this hotel scores a few more points.

This former royal 'jeu de paume', or royal tennis court, was where the active members of Louis XIII's court in the 17th century would meet for a bit of 'game of palm'—so-called because it originated in the 11th century as handball, played by monks bouncing a cork and cloth ball off monastery walls, using their hands as bats.

Seems those first players enjoyed it too much because the Pope at the time banned it, so by the 14th century it had become a game for the nobility only, hence the name of 'royal' tennis. Courts were built at palaces—even one on a 16th-century French ship, it is said.

Along the way, gloves then racquets replaced bare hands and the game morphed into tennis and squash.

Today's hotel surrounds the former court, now called real tennis (www.real-tennis.com) in the UK and Australia, and court tennis in the US, which is enjoying—as you'd expect—a right-royal comeback.

Hotel du Jeu de Paume

54 rue Saint-Louis-en-l'Ile
Paris 75004
FRANCE
Phone: +33 43 26 14 18
info@jeudepaumehotel.com
www.jeudepaumehotel.com/jdp.html

CHALK IT UP

For those with a repressed ambition to become a troglodyte, this is a fabulous place.

For a thousand years, the local inhabitants have carved out homes in the soft chalk cliffs of the Loire River valley. Not only did it save them heaps on building materials, but the 'caves' stayed a steady temperature in summer and were safe from attackers. And were great for keeping the wine cool too.

With all this going for them, you'd think they could hardly be improved, but then someone with a keen eye for business realised that the rooms of this former monastery would scrub up rather nicely as hotel rooms, and installed canopy beds and grand fireplaces.

Now a member of the prestigious Relais & Chateaux group of hotels, these caves make ideal accommodation, while meals and other hotel activities take place in a 18th-century castle nearby, which is interesting too, as its walls are constructed of volcanic 'tuff', used throughout this area. Wannabe cave-dwellers or the already well-heeled—this places caters to both troglodytes and tourists.

Les Hautes Roches

86 quai de la Loire
Rochecorbon Indre-et-Loire 37210
FRANCE
Phone: +33 247 52 88 88
hautesroches@relaischateaux.com
www.leshautesroches.com

DID YOU LEAVE THE TAP ON, DEAR?

This cylindrical structure has had a colourful career—it began in the 19th century as a water tower of course, then became a warehouse, followed by its use as an air-raid shelter during World War II. When windows and two floors were added in 1990, it became one of the world's most unusual hotels, its shape lending itself to curvy lines and circular arches.

Formerly the largest of its kind in Europe, the hotel now has 90 rooms and an 11th floor restaurant with, automatically, 360° views of Cologne.

Hotel im Wasserturm

Kaygasse 2
Cologne 50676
GERMANY
Phone: +49 221 200 80
www.hotel-im-wasserturm.de

The Water Tower

The picture-perfect Water Tower at Bearsted once supplied water to the entire village. Now it sleeps four people in two bedrooms. Its owners must really appreciate unusual buildings as they live nearby in an oast house.

Bearsted ENGLAND
Phone: +44 870 197 1669
www.world-stay.com/en/dist100/13684/
The-Water-Tower-Bearsted.html

And in case you would rather look at water towers than sleep in them:
http://members.tripod.com/~watertowers/decoratedframe.html

MILLING ABOUT

Breeze into this place and get transported back to the days when Matsas worked for its living. Well, as a mill, anyway.

Today its sails are restored, the whitewash sparkling against the blue of the sea and Naoussa harbour. The studios and apartments may appear traditional, but they are up to the minute.

Matsas Windmill

Naoussa, Paros Island,
Aegean
GREECE
Phone: +30 22840 52770
imats@tee.gr
www.greekhotel.com
www.greekislands.com

More windmills:

Windmill Beach House on Buzzards Bay, Massachusetts, USA

www.vrbo.com/vrbo/3843.htm

The Lily Restaurant, (Pictured) Western Australia, AUSTRALIA

http://members.ozemail.com.au/~thelily

The Windmill Hotel, Yorkshire, UK

www.windmill-hotel.co.uk

Le Moulin, Lot et Garonne, FRANCE

www.rentalsfrance.com/moulin

Bradford Old Windmill, Somerset, UK

www.bradfordoldwindmill.co.uk

New Mill, Kent, UK

www.paulharrison.co.uk/newmill/windmill.htm

CHILL OUT ON TOP OF THE WORLD

If the outside temperature is around −35°C, then −10°C seems quite warm by comparison. Especially if you're snuggled up on musk ox fur under an insulating layer of ice—yes, *ice*.

In the higher latitudes, the locals have always used whatever building materials were at hand, usually ice and snow. It would cost nothing, last for months, and be secure and warmer than a regular house. The Ice Hotel's six igloos linked by snow passages are built each December from just snow and water and blend in totally with the snowy landscape outside.

Inside the ice theme continues—an ice bar has ice glasses (or should that be 'ices'?) ice tables, an ice menu, ice seats. Four icy double rooms encircle the lobby and bar. Only the candles have warmth, and their light dances off the sparkling walls.

But this fantasy place, first opened in 1999, only lasts from December until mid-April and is evacuated well before the snow and ice begins to thaw. It is then demolished, then rebuilt late in the year, complete with the guard of hour of ice sculptures in the avenue leading to the entrance.

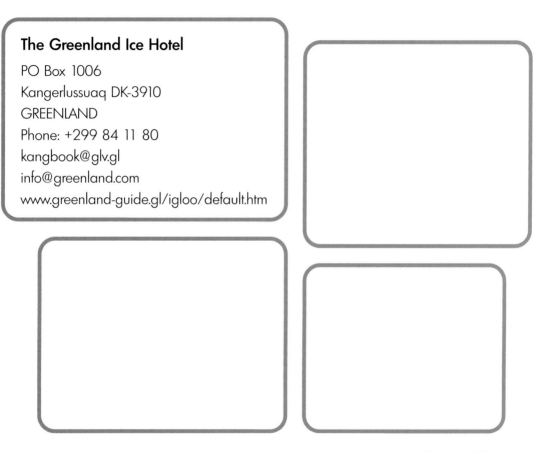

The Greenland Ice Hotel

PO Box 1006
Kangerlussuaq DK-3910
GREENLAND
Phone: +299 84 11 80
kangbook@glv.gl
info@greenland.com
www.greenland-guide.gl/igloo/default.htm

HOLD THAT FORT

Jaisalmer Fort, built in 1156 and for all the world looking like a giant sandcastle, is a teeming, lively warren of Jain temples, shops selling embroidery and fabrics, the seven-storey palace of a former maharaja, private homes and even hotels. It is the oldest living fort in the world, and there are wells within the fort that still provide a regular source of water.

One B&B, the Shreenath Palace, is up several flights of very steep spiral stairs in an old haveli (a traditional townhouse) and has views over almost the entire fort.

But before you start to take notes, the future of the fort is uncertain. Some fear the foundations are crumbling, and there is talk that the inhabitants—around a quarter of Jaisalmer's population— may have to move out.

The fort is 75 metres tall with a 10-metre high sandstone wall, four gateways, and 99 bastions. There are five interconnected palaces, but the sharp twists and turns of the narrow road into the fort have made it invincible.

Let's hope it stays that way.

Shreenath Palace B&B

Jaisalmer Fort B&B
Jaisalmer, Rajasthan
INDIA
Phone: +912 9925 2907
www.indiatravelogue.com/dest/raj/jais.html

NOT FOR SLEEP WALKERS

An ingenious cane lift, which works by hydraulic pressure, is your sole means of reaching your bed for the night, over 26 metres above in the branches of a tree of the Nature Resort. Once there, you could be at ground level, with double beds, an attached bathroom with running water, flushing toilet, and shower, plus a carpeted veranda. No bird ever had a nest as fine as this.

The three tree houses and six eco-lodges of the Nature Resort are located in a pristine tropical rainforest. Before long, guests are assured, they will be moving at rainforest pace, listening to the birds, dodging brilliant butterflies, and inhaling the scent of the forest's many flowers.

Meals are prepared from fruits and vegetables grown in the organic farm, and traditional Kerala dishes are usually served on banana leaves without cutlery.

And if you are wondering about the energy needed to run an eco-lodge, the answer is simple so long as you have some cows. The energy source is a unique combination of solar energy, and gober gas—from cow dung.

Nature Resort

Kerala
INDIA
Phone: +91 4713 30437
http://ecoclub.com/tourindia OR

Green Magic Treehouse Resort

Vythiri, Kerala
INDIA
Phone: +91 487 242055
palmland@vsnl.com
http://travel.vsnl.com/palmland/treehouse

PALATIAL VACATION

It's not often that a royal family invites commoners to share their digs. Yet that is the offer here from a few Indonesian royals. The former Palace of Ubud, home of the last king of Ubud, on the Indonesian island of Bali is grandly empty, save for some remaining members of the royal family who might just happen to hobnob with you in one of the ornate and airy pavilions in the tropical evening air.

There are several simple, clean and affordable rooms available, each with an en-suite, air conditioning or fans, and hot and cold water.

The grand outdoor verandas are where you'll want to hang out, though, cooling off and hoping for a glimpse of the royal clan.

In fact, visitors are welcome to venture into the ornate inner courtyards to see thatched pavilions furnished with heavy Dutch-era armchairs. As a bit of added interest, there are nightly dance performances in the outer courtyard.

We're told that the best pavilion is No. 4, which shares a courtyard with the household of the current head of the family.

Palace of Ubud
(Hotel Puri Saren Agung)

Ubud Main Road, Ubud
Bali, INDONESIA
Phone: +62 361 97 5057
www.indo.com/active/ubud2-1.html

REALLY, TRULLI

Surely one of the strangest towns in the world, Alberobello in southern Italy is full of weird little cone-shaped huts built from local limestone, roofs and all.

Late in the 16th century the aristocracy allowed peasant workers to build houses that could be swiftly dismantled if there was a royal inspection. It was a tax dodge really, as it allowed them to avoid paying the levy for a village.

It was no way for the workers to live, so in 1797 they got together and petitioned the king and received the right to live freely in their trulli. The unusual shape insulates the interior. Alberobello has several huts that may be rented, or there is this one in Fasano near Brindisi. This complex, big enough for six people, has several restored and linked trulli surrounded by grapevines, pine and fig trees, each trullo acting as a separate room.

It's a charming step back into history—a little like sleeping in a time warp.

Trulli houses

Fasano, Puglia
ITALY
Phone: 347 5964148
www.agriturismo.net/la-casa-dei-trulli/index_eng.html
www.alberobello.net

SMALL BUT PERFECTLY FORMED

This is the ideal place to stay—particularly if you are a businessman who has had a little too much sake. Designed as an ultra-cheap place to crash if you have missed the last train home, these cubbyholes are hardly more than a bed, but who cares?

The idea is that men (and, yes, they are often gender-specific) can check-in here, leave their shoes outside and climb into their little bolt-hole, pull the curtains and snooze off the effects of a big night out.

With limited use for travellers, as there is no room in them for luggage, and only a curtain which reduces security, they are still unique in the world, and their name suits them entirely as they are just that—capsules. The moulded plastic capsules are clean and functional, linen is supplied, and some have a pay-per-view TV. If you do have bags, there are central lockers for storage.

While many of the newer ones resemble a line of railway carriage sleeper-ettes, some have several layers, assembled like pigeonholes, and guests neatly post themselves into their individual cavity, rather like an organised filing system for hotel guests.

Capsule Hotels Osaka Minami

American Village in Shinsaibashi, Osaka
JAPAN
Phone: +816 6213 1991
capsule@asahiplaza.co.jp
www.asahiplaza.co.jp/capcel/english.html

HERE'S A BRIGHT IDEA!

While a life as a lighthouse keeper would have its moments, a night or two in a lighthouse is truly an illuminating experience. Definitely recommended if you are a light sleeper.

This Lighthouse at Great Ormes Head is open all year, and is perched 113 metres above the waves crashing around it, five minutes from Llandudno. Choose a room named for its original use—Telegraph, Lamp or Principal Keeper's Suites.

The Lighthouse

Marine Drive
Great Ormes Head
Llandudno LL30 2XD UK
Phone: +441 4928 76819
enquiries@lighthouse-llandudno.co.uk

Other lighthouse stays worldwide include:

Bruce Bay Cottages and Lighthouse (Ontario, CANADA), even available in winter if you have skis or a snowmobile.
www.brucebaycottages.com/Lighthouse.htm

Cantick Head Lighthouse Cottages (Island of Hoy, Orkney, SCOTLAND), an operational lighthouse with self-catering cottages and panoramic views of the Orkney Isles.
www.cantickhead.com

Bengtskär Lighthouse, built in 1906, at 52 metres is the highest lighthouse in the Nordic countries and the first lighthouse museum in Finland. Stay overnight in the old home of the lighthouse keeper.
  www.bengtskar.fi

CHILLY RECEPTIONS

Ice hotels have really taken off worldwide, and although they disappear for summer, they are still pretty cool.

But did you know that in the 1880s in Leadville, Colorado, the USA's largest ice palace was built to bolster a sagging economy? Over 5000 tonnes of ice along with lumber were used in the construction, with the front towers standing 27 metres tall, and most of the walls over nine metres thick.

There was a grand ballroom, a huge icerink, and a riding gallery with a full-sized carousel for children. And every room except the icerink was heated. Despite this bizarre grandeur sadly it closed in 1896.

However, in 1899 the Ice Palace Inn was built on the original site recycling the lumber, and the rooms of today's B&B have been named after the rooms of the original Ice Palace.

Ice Palace Inn Bed & Breakfast

813 Spruce Street
Leadville
Colorado 80461 USA
Phone: 800-754-2840 (in USA)
icepalace@bwn.net
http://icepalaceinn.com

Also look for ice hotels in:
Sweden (www.icehotel.com) *(pictured)*,
Canada (www.icehotel-canada.com),
Alaska (www.chenahotsprings.com/
icehotel.html)

LIGHT RELIEF

It stands to reason that a country like Australia, with such a long and often rugged coast-line (over 36,000 kilometres) should have a correspondingly large number of lighthouses.

And now that many are empty, why not rent them out—especially when many are in such stunning locations? And especially when between May and October guests can have a front row view of migratory whales, as well as sea turtles and dolphins. Guests here are the first to greet the sun each day, as Cape Byron is the most easterly point of mainland Australia.

The Lighthouse Cottages

Byron Bay NSW 2481
AUSTRALIA
www.visitbyronbay.com
phone: +612 6685 6222)

Green Cape Lighthouse Cottages

Ben Boyd National Park
Eden NSW 2551
AUSTRALIA
eden.district@npws.nsw.gov.au
Built in 1883, this is the southernmost lighthouse in the state, and also has NSW's second highest light.

Cape Borda Lightstation
cape.borda@saugov.sa.gov.au

On Kangaroo Island, South Australia, has cottages for rent and fires the restored signal cannon, daily, on the 12:30 pm tour!

Smoky Cape Lighthouse

South West Rocks NSW 2431
AUSTRALIA
www.smokycapelighthouse.com
Enjoy bed and breakfast in the head lighthouse-keeper's former home.

MAN AND BEAST

**William Hill
Man vs Horse Marathon**
Llanwrtyd Wells, Powys LD5 4RS
UK
www.man-v-horse.org.uk
When: mid-June

Wales has laid claim to having the wackiest town in Great Britain—quite a feat, given the eccentricity of the Brits! And it's the former spa-town of Llanwrtyd Wells. This is a bog-snorkelling town—as you've learned—but wait, there's more!

The idea for Llanwrtyd Wells' other main annual event, the Man vs Horse Marathon (held each June) began 25 years ago in a pub, as all good schemes do, when punters at the Neuadd Arms began arguing over the relative strength and stamina of men and horses.

The resulting challenge was a 35 kilometre race run through some of the finest scenery in mid-Wales, with £25,000 in (as yet unclaimed) prize-money for any runner who could beat the fastest horse and rider.

But don't think it's a done deal. In 2003, 400 athletes and 38 horses took part and it was the closest finish yet, with the first athlete coming in just seconds behind the first horse. Apparently in the 18th century, in Cardiganshire, a man beat a horse in a race, but memories are hazy about the length of the course and its terrain. So, maybe the Llanwrtydians' money is safe for a while yet.

HAVE A WILD NIGHT

Dr Doolittle would feel right at home in these places—he could even carry on a conversation late into the night with the animals. But even for regular humans, a night in the zoo has to be an awesome experience.

Victoria's Open Range Zoo at Werribee offers Slumber Safaris—something like a slumber party with lions—every weekend from September to April. Guests enjoy a barbecue and see the animals by spotlight, then stay in a tent overnight at the zoo.

Both Melbourne Zoo and Taronga Zoo in Sydney have Roar'n'Snore programs. At Taronga the experience begins with a night zoo safari by torchlight, peeking at the off-duty animals. You then sleep in a tent with background music provided by those birds and animals that stay awake all night.

Melbourne Zoo (phone: +613 9285 9355) www.zoo.org.au

Taronga Zoo (phone: +612 9969 2777) www.zoo.nsw.gov.au

Western Plains Zoo in Dubbo, NSW (www.zoo.nsw.gov.au, enquiries@zoofari.com.au) has a permanent Zoofari Lodge with private African-style canvas covered rooms, so visitors can stay overnight in comfort.

Werribee Zoo Park

K Road
Werribee Victoria 3030
AUSTRALIA
Phone: +613 9731 9600
vorz@zoo.org.au
www.zoo.org.au

CONVERSATION ICE-BREAKER

Cruises come in all shapes and sizes, but few would be stranger than this one. From December to the end of April you can join the *Sampo*, a 75-metre icebreaker as it ploughs through 50 centimetres of thick ice, and speeds over eight-metre thick ice banks. Cruises last from two to six hours and are ideal for groups or conferences. On board there are restaurants and lounges, and even a shop.

The trip begins with a reindeer safari or a thrilling snow-mobile ride, and the super-hardy may choose a quick dip in the Gulf of Bothnia while on the cruise—if they're game.

Once owned by the Finnish government, for 30 years the *Sampo* was invaluable in helping to keep the northern shipping lanes open. Now it is the world's most unusual cruiser, and the only passenger ice-breaker in the world.

Cruise times vary depending on the time of year, and may include overnight stops at ice camp sites or in fishing lodges. Temperature during all this? As low as −40°C.

Sampo, Russian Ice-breaker

Torikatu 2, Kemi
Lapland 94100
FINLAND
Phone: +358 16 256 548
Sampo@kemi.fi
www.sampotours.com/eng/arktinenseik.html

Roche

Weird and Wacky · 75

ICE DREAM

If you think simply being at latitude 63° South, surrounded by icebergs is adventurous enough, try this.

Make sure you take the chance to sleep in a 'mummy' bag (a sarcophagus-shaped sleeping bag) on Antarctica itself—right on the ice, insulated only by a sleeping mat.

Peregrine Adventures takes several tours each summer to both the Arctic and Antarctic on specially adapted polar ships, the *Akademik Ioffe/Peregrine Mariner* and the *Akademik Sergei Vavilov/Peregrine Voyager*.

Passengers scoot around the icebergs the size of office blocks in rubber Zodiacs, and get up close and personal with penguins and seals. But the (ice) cap of the trip is to say you have spent a night actually *on* Antarctica. The second thing many brag about is stripping down and swimming in the warm water of the sunken caldera at Deception Island with steam rising from the black sands. It's an active volcano, so make it a quick dip.

Oh, and get some pictures. No-one's going to believe you otherwise!

Peregrine Adventures

258 Lonsdale Street
Melbourne Vic. 3000
AUSTRALIA
Phone: +613 9663 8611
websales@peregrine.net.au
www.peregrine.net.au/antarctica/index.asp

LIGHTHOUSE-KEEPING

One Welsh lighthouse has had a strange history of its own. Built on an island in 1821, since then the land has been reclaimed and it now stands at the end of a stony peninsula instead.

It's a squat lighthouse, decommissioned in 1922, with walls over 60 centimetres thick. The rooms are wedge-shaped because, of course, the building is circular, and the flat top makes an ideal spot for barbecues or for watching sunsets—or sunrises. The lighthouse still even has the original indoor well, built to collect rainwater.

Meanwhile, in Scotland, Corsewall Light, built in 1815 and now automated, still flashes to warn ships at the entrance to Loch Ryan. It has been transformed into a luxury hotel and restaurant, and only the copper knick-knacks and paintings remain to remind guests of the valuable service it has performed over the years, guiding ships safely into the harbour.

West Usk Lighthouse

Lighthouse Road
St Brides Wentlooge
Newport, Gwent, NP10 8SF
WALES
Phone: +44 1633 810 126/+44 1633 815 860
lighthouse1@tesco.net
www.westusklighthouse.co.uk

Corsewall Lighthouse

Kirkcolm, Stranraer,
SCOTLAND DG9 0QG
Phone: +44 1776 853 220
corsewall-lighthouse@msn.com
www.lighthousehotel.co.uk

FRUITY FOLLY

North of Airth, near Falkirk in Scotland, stands a truly bizarre folly. Built in 1761 and shaped like a pineapple (yes, really) it stands fourteen metres high. This piece of whimsy was originally created as Dunmore House's garden retreat—a summerhouse—and no doubt was the height of architectural daring in its day.

Strange as it appears, it seems to have been carefully planned as each 'leaf' of the pineapple is so designed to drain water to prevent frost damage. But why a pineapple? Apparently these had been grown as an exotic fruit in hothouses in Scotland around the early 18th century and may even have been raised on this estate—even in this building.

What is more interesting is that the workmen's quarters in the octagonal tower crowned by the pineapple is administered by the Landmark Trust, and is available as exclusive—albeit eccentric—holiday accommodation. Dunmore House has extensive gardens and is open daily all year, but why settle for only seeing it in visiting hours when you can move in and live under a pineapple?

The Pineapple Summerhouse

Dunmore House
Falkirk
SCOTLAND
Phone: +44 1324 831 137
info@landmarktrust.co.uk
information@nts.org.uk
www.landmarktrust.org

FREE TO STAY IN JAIL

Ironically located in the Free State, the Philippolis Old Jail, built in 1872, has recently opened its doors to willing (and paying) residents. You can still certainly get the feel, though, of how it must have felt to be locked up here in the jail's heyday.

The almost soundproof cells are simple and self-catering and are just two metres by three metres, while the walls are 60 centimetres thick, making them cool in summer and warm in winter. But there is no way you could you have dug your way out or passed through those hefty wood and steel doors, which today open easily.

And if you have developed a taste for high-security accommodation, the Old Jail in Grahamstown might also appeal. Guests may book into two, three, or six-person cells, but these days there is no curfew. And the only key in the door is yours.

Philippolis Old Jail

Justisie Street
Philippolis, Free State
SOUTH AFRICA
Phone: +27 11 973 1778
info@wheretostay.co.za
www.wheretostay.co.za/oldjail/default.htm

Old Jail Backpackers

40 Somerset Street
Grahamstown
SOUTH AFRICA
Phone: +27 46 636 1001
oldjail@imaginet.co.za
www.grahamstown.co.za/
accomodation_budget.asp

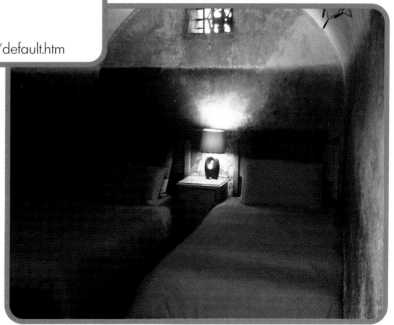

WITHERING HEIGHTS

One thing is certain, Mr Flowerdew would never recognise the place today. In the late 1870s, Flowerdew had been the highest bidder when the British government sold this land to be used as a tea plantation in the mountainous 'hill country' of Sri Lanka, then Ceylon.

In the 1930s the hilltop was levelled and a tea factory was built. Its height captured every whiff of breeze so essential for the drying—or withering—of the fresh tea shoots, and for over 40 years it produced some of the best of Ceylon's teas.

Today the 'withering lofts' have been converted into comfortable bedrooms, and the huge engine that once powered the factory stands in the entrance lobby under the original overhead line shaft.

The climate here is cool and refreshing. 'Bring a sweater', is the repeated caution, and at an elevation of 2072 metres, just 193 kilometres from Colombo, it provides essential respite from Sri Lanka's steamy coastal heat.

And, of course, there are tea-making facilities—with fine Ceylon tea—in each room, plus instructions on how to make the perfect cuppa.

Tea Factory

Nuwara Eliya
SRI LANKA

Phone: +941 433 755, +941 326 767
info@dilmahtea.com

www.aitkenspencehotels.com/teafactory

MAKE A BREAK FOR IT

This former Crown Prison, built on Sweden's seventh-largest island, has relatively recently (in 1975) hung up its handcuffs, when the last prisoner was discharged. But today the switch to comfy hotel is complete.

Cells still have heavy doors, but no bars on the windows, and come with ensuites and cable TV, while the exercise yard now has a delightful cafe and a space to play boules!

And the meals—well let's say bread and water is available, but much more is on the menu at the restaurant housed in a 1670-built residence. Appropriately the hotel's pub bar, Finken, translates as 'the Nick'.

The central gallery once used for observation of the prisoners now works beautifully as a light-filled atrium.

Langholmen Hotel

Gamla Kronohaktet
Langholmsmuren 20, Stockholm
SWEDEN
Phone: +468 720 8500
hotell@langholmen.com
www.langholmen.com/indexEn.html

By way of escape, the hotel offers special evenings where guests may try to break out of jail, solve a century-old murder mystery, or even stand trial. It's all in good fun and even if found guilty, they know their sentence will only last a couple of hours.

This is the only way have a jail break. With your own set of keys.

COOL COMFORT

'Throw your tumblers on the floor after you have skolled the vodka' is the unusual advice from the proprietors of this hotel. They don't mind a bit because the tumbler is made of ice, and the floor is ice. What's more, the walls and the roof and even the beds are made of ice.

Located above the Arctic Circle, 68° North, the complex is freshly carved from 1000 tonnes of ice and 2000 tonnes of snow every winter, and opens around mid-December, then melts away around May.

There are guestrooms, a chapel, conference facilities, a golf room and of course the highly popular Absolut-Ice bar. Temperatures stay between 4°C and 9°C but guests are often surprised how warm they can be in thermal sleeping bags, snuggled down in soft reindeer skins on an iceblock bed.

In the morning, there's hot lingonberry juice, and rather than warming up in front of a blazing fire, there is the sauna, or more traditional cleansing, such as showers, at the Jukkasjärvi Holiday Cabins next door. Or they choose a snowmobile safari, go dog-sledding—or simply chill out.

Ice Hotel

981 91 Jukkasjärvi, Lapland
SWEDEN
Phone: +46 980 66 800
info@icehotel.com
www.icehotel.com

PARKING SPACE

This one-person hotel, opened in 1998, has to be the smallest in the world. As if this is not enough, it is also perched thirteen metres above the ground in the branches of an oak tree, accessible by a long ladder, in the central park of Vasteras, about 100 kilometres west of Stockholm. Artist Mikael Genberg, the creator of the project, says, 'I didn't have any knowledge of climbing and very little about building so it was quite an adventure.'

The hotel is just 12.5 square metres, with two balconies, a furnished bedroom, toilet, and kitchenette. While some guests are a little unsure of what to do once they arrive, most relish the bizarre situation.

Initially, people could stay in the treehouse for free, but as interest grew, Genberg decided to charge guests for the privilege. There are two packages—Hotell Hackspett Bohéme (bring your own sheets and food) or HH DeLuxe with supper and breakfast provided (raised in a basket), and linen supplied.

The house and guest become a sort of installation art for people walking below in the park, and this suits Gensberg. 'The guest becomes something of an actor in a strange role play,' he says.

Hotell Hackspett (Woodpecker Hotel)

VasaparkenVasteras
SWEDEN
Phone: +46 70 775 5393
mikael@konst.org
www.konst.org/genberg/engtext.htm

UTTERLY AMAZING

From the amazing mind and hands of the creator of the Woodpecker Hotel, Mikael Genberg, comes this unique brainwave.

Swedish people love their white-gabled red summerhouses—and he has taken the Otter Inn one step further. Not content to be lakeside, the Otter Inn is really *in* Lake Malaren, with the sleeping area completely submerged.

The watertight bedroom is 3 metres below the water with panoramic windows to take in the passing aquatic life. Or rather, as the artist-creator likes to imagine it, 'You are in an aquarium—for fish to be beholders of man.' Local boats often make a couple of passes, just to catch a glimpse.

Gensberg has an esoteric take on all this, calling it the tendency to 'transform the experience of fear to an experience of love'. If that seems a bit deep—think of it as taking the very real risk of sleeping underwater and turning it into a liberating feat. Guests of the inn are taken by boat to the inn then left to enjoy the peace and solitude. Select the deluxe version and supper will be delivered later.

You can swim, sunbathe, or paddle your inflatable canoe to a nearby island. You may even sight an otter!

Utter Inn (Otter Inn)

Vasteras
SWEDEN
mikael@konst.org
www.konst.org/genberg/engtext.htm

SUBTERRANEAN MEDITERRANEAN

Cappadoccia is honeycombed with underground settlements. There are around 200 of them, but their history is hazy. Some say they evolved from prehistoric shelters, other scholars date them as originating at the end of the 4th century BC. Some think the Hittites may been behind their excavation, using them as secret tunnels for defence.

Byzantine bits and pieces from the 5th to 10th centuries have been found, so it is likely they were used by Ottoman sultans and their court as cool boltholes away from the scorching summer sun that bakes the ground solid in this region.

Some believe the settlements were used by early Christians in the 7th century as refuges. But whether they were originally meant as escapes or military bases, today these places, open from April to October, are just as popular with tourists as they have been through the ages.

Yunak Evleri, Ürgrüp

Cappadocia
TURKEY
yunak@yunak.com
www.cappadociaonline.com/under.html

Esbelli Evi, Ürgrüp

Cappadocia
TURKEY
Phone: +90 384 341 3395
suha@esbelli.com.tr
www.esbelli.com

WHAT A LEGEND!

Kokopelli is the mythical Native American minstrel often sketched on rocky high places. Little wonder then that this cave, blasted into the sandstone cliff in 1980, bears his name. Designed as an appropriately rocky office for a geologist, 21 metres below the surface, three holes were drilled into the cave for ventilation, electrical lines, and a chimney. For a while the owners lived here but the space morphed into a luxury B&B in 1997.

Located near the Mesa Verde National Monument on the intersection of four states—the Four Corners area—the views from the cave 85 metres above the La Plata River and cliff tops are magic. Sunsets are said to be amazing. But don't expect a standard front door. The entrance is located in the cliff face and the cave is then reached via a path, steps and finally a short ladder.

The one-bedroom cave home is furnished South-western style and has a cascading water-fall-like shower—even a flagstone hot tub. Which would give Kokopelli himself something to really sing and dance about.

Kokopelli's Cave B&B

206 W 38th Street
Farmington New Mexico 87401
US
Phone: +150 5325 7855
kokoscave@hotmail.com
www.bbonline.com/nm/kokopelli

THE LITTLE ENGINE THAT DID

It's not often you can book into a piece of popular history, but here you can eat dinner in the Chattanooga Choo Choo's elegant Victorian-era dining car, then sleep onboard an authentic restored train carriage.

Only the rich and famous could afford this style of private travel across America in 1900. Today this train goes nowhere, but the comfort has certainly improved with a queen-size bed.

The coming of the rail line brought prosperity to Chattanooga making it an important stop during the golden age of railroads. The Terminal Station was erected in 1908, and the first train pulled into the platform in 1909.

The station stood empty after the line's closure in 1970, but now after millions of dollars spent to refurbish it and create a 12-hectare vacation and convention complex, it has again become central to the city. The station's magnificent dome, now restored, graces the dining hall, and original carriages have returned to use for accommodation and dining.

And of course, the Chattanooga Choo Choo's wood-burning engine—the same one used on the first run south from Cincinnati to Chattanooga in 1880 and last used in the 1940s—has pride of place.

Chattanooga Choo Choo

Market Street
Chattanooga, Tennessee
US
frontdesk@choochoo.com
www.choochoo.com

BRANCH OFFICES

Got the nesting instinct? Then these two places could be real love nests. The Nahiku Tree house on the east coast of the island of Maui is over eight metres above the ground in a huge mango tree. From the treehouse's deck you can see from the Pacific on one side to Maui's volcano on the other.

The sleeping loft with ladder access sleeps two, while bathroom facilities are at ground level. You may even grill your dinner on the deck among the leaves.

Then, there's the treehouse in a state park, over fifteen metres up a giant cedar tree, allowing guests views of Mt Rainier from their beds. But you'd better be fit because a suspension footbridge through the cedar rainforest leads to a five-storey staircase. And at the top, your little nest. Well, not so little—the building has a sleeping loft with two double beds, bathroom, kitchen and dining area, plus an observation room, which you'll need because those views just go on forever.

Nahiku Tree House

380 Nahiku Road
Maui
HAWAII
380 NahikuRoad@nahiku.com
www.nahiku.com

Cedar Creek Treehouse and Observatory

Mt Rainier
UNITED STATES
(PO Box 204, Ashford WA 98304)
Phone: +136 0569 2991
treehouse@mashell.com
www.cedarcreektreehouse.com

THE LIGHTNESS OF BEING

Two islands called The Brothers mark the east side of San Pablo Strait in San Francisco Bay, opposite two similar islands, The Sisters. Part gingerbread house, part seaside cottage, the East Brother Light Station, that went into operation in March 1874, is operated by a non-profit corporation for the benefit of the public.

The lighthouse is built of wood, but the spaces between the studs on the outside walls are filled with bricks. The cosy bedrooms in the historic lighthouse are in the former lighthouse keeper's quarters. Each room has a queen-sized bed and, as you'd expect, a magnificent view of the Bay. Walter's Quarters is smaller and is located in the fog signal building.

You must remember to keep your luggage down when staying as you'll need both hands and some strength to climb from the boat that brings you here and then up the 3.6-metre vertical ladder.

Oh, and you need to like foghorns. Between October and April they can sound at any time, day or night.

East Brother Light Station

117 Park Place
Point Richmond CA 94801
UNITESD STATES
Phone: + 151 0233 2385
ebls@earthlink.net
www.ebls.org

OUT OF YOUR TREE

Here's how to be out of your tree, and still in it. This bizarre house built in 1990 in a concrete pseudo-tree was designed by Dang Viet Nga, the daughter of Truong Chinh, former president of the Socialist Republic of Vietnam, and known as Hang Nga, who studied architecture and lived for many years in Moscow.

The locals call it the crazy house, and it certainly is, well, avant garde!

Each room is themed: the Bird Room with an eagle perched on an egg-shaped fireplace, the Gourd Room, and even a Kangaroo Room. Beds are mirrored and curtained off, and as for the furniture—let's say each piece is a work of art. Right down to the finely carved knobs and handles.

Some bathrooms have curved baths wrapped along the wall, and all have showers. Bedside reading lamps may have started life as gourds, and local artefacts such as stuffed animal heads and baskets are also on display.

It's all very spidery, from the house's shape to the plastic spiders dangling outside in a wire web over the pond, where you can take afternoon tea.

Or you may enjoy it in the 20 metre giraffe-shaped tearoom nearby. Yes, really!

**The Spider Web Chalet
—Hang Nga Tree House**
Dalat
VIETNAM
Phone: +841 632 2070

CHEUNG CHAU BUN FESTIVAL

Imagine a tower of sticky pink and white buns! No evil spirit worth its reputation would stick around long, would it? And that's just what the inhabitants of Cheung Chau Island off Hong Kong want.

The custom goes back a long way—to the Qing Dynasty a couple of centuries ago, when islanders were struck by a mighty storm, along with the double whammy of a virus that left them reeling. To them it was a sign from above, and since then they have used this rather sweet way of making amends with the spirit world.

Each year, on Buddha's birthday in late May, thousands of steaming buns filled with lotus-paste are assembled as tempting treats on three sixteen-metre bamboo 'bun-towers' outside the Pak Tai temple. In this fishing community, the deal (they ask) is that their boats will be protected and a good season ensured. An effigy is burned before the buns are hungrily devoured.

Cheung Chau Bun Festival

Cheung Chau, Hong Kong
CHINA
info@cheungchau.org
www.cheungchau.org
When: late May

WIFE CARRYING FESTIVAL

Wives in Finland are no doubt glad to be participating in this festival in this era. In the 19th century when the custom originated, they might have been soundly subdued first, before being dragged off to the brigand's home base.

Today, it's all done in fun. You don't even have to BYO wife—any female over 17 years old will do. And although you may snatch someone else's wife, the expectation is that you'll give her back afterwards.

There are even strict rules for the event. The 'wife's' weight must be at least 49 kilograms. There is a 253.5 metre course with various surfaces, plus dry and water-based obstacles. And one of the official rules is that all the participants must have fun.

Dropping and bouncing of the wife will incur a fine, and while negotiating this course with a wife who is a little on the, er, cuddly side might seem a liability, the reward, if you win, is sobering.

Or not! The prize is your wife's weight in beer.

Wife Carrying Festival

Rutakontie 21 FIN-74300, Sonkajärvi
FINLAND
Fax: +358 1727 27106
eukonkanto@sonkajarvi.fi
www.sonkajarvi.fi
When: early July

LYING FOR THE SAKE OF IT

The residents of a town in France have plenty to boast about. So much so that they get together each year to practice, and reward it at the Liar's Festival. Moncrabeau even has a signposted Liar's Circuit as well as the Academie des Menteurs (liars), established in 1748, which welcomes 'liars, boasters, storytellers and other idle persons expert in the art of untruthfulness'.

On the first Sunday each August the locals get together see who can tell the tallest tale in front of 40 Academy officials. The finest fibber is then crowned and seated on the Liar's Throne.

Across the Channel in England, each November the World's Biggest Liar Competition takes place at The Bridge Inn, Santon Bridge, in Cumbria, and one recent tale, for example, detailed how the Lake District was formed by moles and eels rather than glacial action. The competition began with a renowned local confabulationist, 19th-century publican Will Ritson, whose tall tales inspired others to massage the truth for maximum effect.

Liar's Festival

Moncrabeau, FRANCE
Phone: +335 53 65 43 27
tourisme@crt.cr-aquitaine.fr
www.crt.cr-aquitaine.fr/index-us.asp
When: early August

Whitehaven Civic Hall

Lowther Street
Whitehaven, Cumbria CA28 7SH UK
Tel: +441 9468 52821
civichalls@copelandbc.gov.uk
When: November

ORANGE-AID

More than eight centuries ago, in Italy, a serious local revolt took place and the outraged citizens hurled stones at the ruler's troops. Things have evolved over the years and now it's the Battle of the Oranges instead, with nearly 200 of these festivals having been held in this tiny village in Piedmont.

And just in case you think this is an awful waste of good food (which it is), the argument is that Italy grows too many oranges and the excess must be destroyed under EEC rules.

With true Italian flair the teams elected to do the throwing are decked out in red hats and brilliant medieval uniforms with a handy pouch for storing the yet-to-be-thrown fruit. Those representing the ancient tyrant are hauled through the streets on horse-drawn trucks, and are well protected. A swift, well-aimed orange can hurt!

The good news is, you don't have to be a local if you visit during the five-day festival. You can become an impromptu orange launcher and put your own new spin on orange squash!

Il Carnevale d'Ivrea, Ivrea, Piedmonte

ITALY
Phone: +39 125 641 521
info@carnevalediivrea.it
www.carnevale.ivrea.it/defaulteng.asp
When: early February

CABBAGE CONTEST

Who could have imagined it? A festival totally devoted to fermented cabbage!

Kimchi, that love-it-or-hate-it staple turns up at every meal in Korea. But did you know that there are around 160 varieties? Visit Korea in October and you can see (and sample) most of them at the Kimchi Festival.

This festival is held at various cities around the Republic of Korea, and the format for each is generally the same—a massive exhibition, information booths and contests. How can you have a kimchi-making contest? Simple. Teams combine to create the spiciest, fieriest, tastiest combo of chilli paste and Chinese cabbage, carefully massaging the spice mix between the leaves.

Visitors can also have a turn and end up with their hands stinging from the chillies— or maybe a prize. Kimchi is reputed to have definite health benefits. Some locals ate great quantities during the 2003 SARs outbreak and credited their survival to it. Seoul, Korea's capital, even has a Kimchi museum filled with kimchi-abilia, located at the ASEM Convention Center in Samsung-dong.

Kim Chi Festival,

KOREA

einfo@mail.knto.or.kr
www.knto.or.kr/eng/hallyu/kimchi.html
When: October

MUD STICKS

Playing with mud as a small child is acceptable. Even coating yourself with it in the pursuit of beauty is okay. But doing it in public, as an adult? Korea's annual Poryong Mud Festival each summer allows people to unleash the inner (messy) child in order to get their outer adult bodies looking good again. At least that's the theory of it.

In practice there are a lot of contests and activities—whole body mud packs, mud body painting and massages, mud beauty contests. Even a mud sculpture contest. Evidently the mud from this area is rich with minerals essential for good skin health. It helps circulation, and may (let's hurry to Poryong!) reduce wrinkles.

This hope keeps people coming back and layering on the mud so the goodness can soak into the skin. That and the fun of being on the beach with everyone else enjoying themselves the same way.

Poryong Mud Festival

Taecheon Beach
Poryong City, Ch'ungch'ongnam-do Province
KOREA
Phone: +8245 2930 3541
Fax: +8245 2930 3784
poryong@soback.kornet.nm.kr
When: July

THOROUGHLY HOOKED

Not for the squeamish, this one. And if you have trouble looking at your teenager's piercings, then this is certainly not for you. Each year, to celebrate the triumph of good over evil, Hindu devotees take part in this amazing religious event. Not content with merely carrying burdens up the 276 steps to the Batu caves, many choose to dangle them from skewers and steel rods inserted through their cheeks, lips or tongue.

Some people wear a kavadi, weighing up to 23 kilograms—a sort of metal harness, anchored to the shoulders with steel hooks. Yes, it is confronting! If it helps, you should know that those taking part say they feel no pain. They have been psyching themselves up to it for days and are in a trance.

The date for this popular festival—which can draw as many as a million onlookers and devotees—varies between January and February. A complicated calculation sees it falling on the full moon day in the Tamil month of Thai when the astrological star, Pusam, reigns.

Most importantly, although bizarre, this event is not a sideshow act. It is a sincere religious experience for those involved.

Thaipusam

Batu Caves
Kuala Lumpur
MALAYSIA
www.tourism.gov.my
When: January/February

RADISHINGLY BEAUTIFUL

Now, it's entirely likely that radish-carving has never been high on your list of must-see activities. Yet in this Mexican city, one day each year, everything comes up radishes. Or is that radishes are coming up everything else? Because you'll find radishes honed into flowers, people, animals and much more.

There are nativity scenes, which is appropriate because it is held on 23 December each year, and also because the tradition has a religious basis, going back to colonial times when missionaries taught the locals how to cultivate radishes.

It all happens in the Oaxaca's central square and, of course, the fun doesn't stop with the multitudes of radishes on display, amazing as they are. Expect fireworks, music and dancing, and stalls selling buñuelos, deep-fried donuts soaked in sugar syrup. Plus piñatas—those fragile Mexican gourds packed with gifts—that you have to smash to win.

And if you enjoy that, then it is also tradition to smash the dish that has held your donut to show your fortune for the coming year.

Noche de Rábanos (Radish Night)

Oaxaca Tourist Office
5 de Mayo, Avenida Morelos
Colonía Centro 68000 Oaxaca
MEXICO
Phone: +52 9516 4828
info@oaxaca.gob.mx
http://oaxaca-travel.com
When: 23 December

HOLI WATER

Those from the Indian subcontinent are known for their love of bright colours, but whoever heard of throwing paint over people? The Nepalese people don't call it paint. It's coloured water, they say, and the festival is deeply founded in Hindu myth dating to the time when Lord Krishna is said to have teased some village maidens by throwing coloured water over them. So if you are planning to be in Nepal during the February–March full moon, pack some old clothes so you can enter into the fun of it all—get completely splashed with 'coloured' water and make sure you throw plenty back!

Nepal Tourist Office

Bhrikuti Mandap
Kathmandu
NEPAL
Phone: +977 1256 909 or +977 1256 229
info@ntb.wlink.com.np
When: February/March full moon

And then there's Songkran in April, Thailand's wet and wild festival. Here they use coloured powder and clay as well as water, so you will likely get completely drenched as well as tinted and daubed. This time it's to celebrate New Year, but it looks for all the world like just a good excuse for some harmless mayhem.

Songkran Water Festival

various places in Thailand
THAILAND
www.thailandgrandfestival.com
When: April

WHERE ELSE BUT THE UK?

Up-Helly-Aa

Lerwick, Shetland
SCOTLAND
info@visitshetland.com
When: January

A fire festival in midwinter, with Viking overtones. Flaming torches, bonfires, ancient fur-trimmed costumes, partying and parades. The last Tuesday in January is the best and brightest.

Cheese Rolling

Cooper's Hill, Gloucester UK
cheeserolling@msn.com
www.cheese-rolling.co.uk
When: last weekend in May

There may be hundreds of ways to use cheese, but whoever thought of bowling it down a hill? Here the aim is to roll a seven pound (that's just over three kilograms) cheese 300 metres down a very steep hill and not end up at the bottom with it. Winners get to keep their battered cheese.

World Toe Wrestling

Ye Olde Royal Oak Inn
Wetton, Derbyshire UK
brian.holmes@talk21.com
www.dcfg.fsnet.co.uk/toewrestling/Index.htm
When: late June

This must have been a beer-coaster idea. In 1976, the Wetton punters dreamt up a new sport. Toe wrestling involves locking big toes, attempting to force the opponent's foot to the rails. Sadly it was not selected as an Olympic sport when the organisers applied in 1997. Maybe next time.

World Coal Carrying Championship

Royal Oak
Owl Lane Gawthorpe, Yorkshire UK
steve@stonesandco.freeserve.co.uk
www.gawthorpe.ndo.co.uk
When: Easter Monday

Where else but here—and what else but coal in this mining district? King of the Coil Humpers (aka champion coal carrier) is the crown to be won, the strange contest triggered by a dare between two men in 1963. The current men's record for humping a hundred-weight (around 50 kilograms) of coal just over a kilometre is four minutes six seconds.

Just try it!

World Gurning Contest

Phone: +441 9468 21554
lakestay@globalnet.co.uk
www.whitehaven.org.uk/gurn.html
When: Saturday in mid-September

As sweet relief from beauty pageants, here is one contest where ugly wins. Crab apples grown here are sour enough to make you screw your face up—so why not celebrate the season with a face-pulling (gurning) fair? A Crab Fayre, as it's called. To make it worse, you also have to do it wearing a horse collar.

World Stinging Nettle Challenge

The Bottle Inn
Marshwood, Dorset UK
Phone: +441 2976 78254
thebottleinn@msn.com
www.thebottleinn.co.uk
When: Mid June

It's what it sounds like. The lads get together and eat nettles—up to 70 at a stretch. They also compete to see who has grown the longest nettle. The record stands at 4.75 metres.

BOWLING DOWN THE ROAD

If you happen to be out driving one fine Sunday along a country road in West Cork, you may find the road blocked by a group of men in caps and tracksuits heaving an iron ball down the tarmac, and having a fine good time of it. And, unlike many diversions in this part of the world, this one didn't begin as a bright idea in a pub.

Road bowling started, many believe, in ancient Ulster, at Eamhain Maca near Armagh. The kings of Ireland lived here, and another royal, Prince William of Orange, also seemed to enjoy the sport of heaving a ball along the road. Some say the pharaohs weren't averse to it either.

Although stone balls were once used, a 58 millimetre, 8 kilogram, cast-iron ball is now the preference, the aim being to cover a prescribed distance with a set number of throws.

And far from being a casual collection of lads throwing a ball, there is a controlling body—Bol Chumann na h-Eireann—and set rules. And international affiliations with the UK, US, Holland, Italy and Germany and participating in European championships have taken the sport to new heights. Or is that lengths?

Road Bowling

West Cork
IRELAND
barabas_o_r@yahoo.com
www.roadbowls.8m.com

LA TOMATINA

Bad entertainers sometimes expect the tomatoes to fly, but in this little town 30 kilometres from Valencia you can find yourself covered in red juice for apparently no reason.

There is one, of course. You will have lucked-in on the annual tomato festival—La Tomatina, which officially honours the town's patron saint—held at the height of the season when the tomatoes are at their squishy ripest. It's a free-for-all, and the juicy red fruit really flies. But no, this is not a pagan tribute to the tomato gods.

La Tomatina, Buñol

SPAIN

tomatina@lahoya.net

www.lahoya.net

When: last Wednesday of August

Seems it simply stems from an argument in the 1940s when tempers heated and the nearest missiles at hand were tomatoes. Today it's a good excuse to let off steam and throw things about. Truckloads of tomatoes, as it happens.

The plaza's shopfronts cover up as soon as the missiles appear, and then the fun begins. The messy festa only lasts a couple of hours, and then it's back to the other more serious parts of the celebrations—eating and drinking, dancing and singing.

WHAT A LOT OF BULL!

At eight o'clock every morning for a week around 7 July, the bulls of Pamplona are let out to play with the people. Or that's what they think, perhaps. If you have a desire to raise your adrenaline, then this is the place for you. There is nothing quite like seeing a herd of 600 kilogram bulls charging at you to get the blood pumping.

Unfortunately, over the years, some have found their own blood exiting their bodies after coming too close to a pair of horns. Sadly, many have been injured, or died in the history of the event.

The running of the bulls is the showiest—and let's face it, the most newsworthy—part of the annual Fiesta of San Fermin. It makes great television to see these massive animals charging almost a kilometre through a town, past rows of cheering people, then into the bullring, especially when they appear to be chasing a bunch of (mostly) young men who are running as if their lives depended on it. Which they do.

It's a risk-taker's paradise and anyone can join in. Many do, without a qualm. And it's especially fine if you survive it.

San Fermin—Running of the Bulls
Pamplona
SPAIN
fermin@sanfermin.com
www.sanfermin.com
When: seven days from 7 July each year

PLAN A WET WEDDING

Underwater Wedding Ceremony

Trang Chamber of Commerce,
Koh Kradan, Trang
THAILAND
Phone: +66 7521 0238,
      +66 7522 5353
underwater_wedding@yahool.com
www.underwaterwedding.com

Attention all those who want a wedding with a difference: Must be able to dive. Willing to share the special day with up to 40 other couples. Guests are optional.

The Trang Underwater Wedding Ceremony started in 2000 and has become a tradition, with lovers tying the knot in the deep. Interestingly, although this ceremony could hardly be more unusual, it still manages to preserve some aspects of a traditional Thai wedding.

The wedding procession to receive the bridal dowry is emulated by 500-strong speedboat convoy, flag festooned for the occasion. On Koh Kradan Island, after a blessing ceremony, the couples dive to the spot where they will marry surrounded by brilliant coral reef fish. While it is not for everyone—only couples who are both certified divers are allowed to take part, of course—it certainly adds new meaning to 'taking the plunge'.

DEEP SLEEP

This world first (and only) underwater hotel, opened in 1986, is also a scientific base, used since the early 1970s as a research laboratory to explore the continental shelf off the coast of Puerto Rico. It must be something in the water here, because there are always proposals. Underwater weddings follow, naturally complete with the world's only underwater wedding cake, and often unexpected 'guests' such as passing fish and other divers outside the windows witness the ceremony.

While you must be able to scuba dive to reach this strange hotel, guests can continue to dive once there. Of course the rooms are watertight, with their own air supply. A three-hour diver training class is available so guests who are not certified divers can qualify, and there is also complete dive certification and specialty training.

Jules' Undersea Lodge

Key Largo Undersea Park
Key Largo, Florida USA
Phone: +1 305 451 2353
info@jul.com
www.jul.com

DIZZY DANCING

Feel you are going around in circles? Your life is a whirl? It's not new. These members of the Sufi Mevlevi Order trace their roots to 13th-century Konya in the Central Anatolia Region of Turkey. Each year, in the first half of December, the order commemorates the death of their founder, Mevlana Celaleddin Rumi.

The spinning or 'sema' of the white-robed dancers—all males, popularly known as Whirling Dervishes—is almost hypnotic, and is a great tourist attraction.

But, however photogenic it may be, the word is that this is not solely for show. The participants see these mystical gyrations as an honour to their great teacher, as well as a means of having union with God.

Even the outfits are symbolic: the hat (a gravestone), the cloak (a coffin) and the white skirt (a shroud). The dance movements themselves are meant to represent the orbits of celestial bodies around the sun.

No one admits to head spins after the dance, of course, but even for onlookers it can be a dizzying experience.

Whirling Dervishes Festival

Ismet Inonu Bulvar 5
Banceliever, Ankara
TURKEY
Phone: +903 12 212 8300
turizm.bilgi.islem@sim.net.tr
www.tourismturkey.org
When: December

LOOK MUM, NO PASSPORT

Australia is a bit light-on for local royalty, so a visit to the Hutt River Province is a must if you want to meet a home-grown prince and his royal court. Prince Leonard George Casley was a wheat farmer until late-1969 when the government sent him a letter that changed his life—and ultimately resulted in a new landlocked country within a country.

Casley regarded the wheat quota he received as unacceptable, and so he did the only respectable thing he felt a farmer could do in the situation. He decided to leave the country. But not physically. He chose to secede, and in 1970, his property became his kingdom—The Hutt River Province—and he and his family upped their status to become the new rulers.

This 75-square kilometre province is located north of Perth, the capital of Western Australia, in pleasant countryside. As the prince expected, tourists love to visit his unusual country to buy souvenirs, stamps, coins and licence plates, and visit the chapel and the various monuments. Then they return to Australia.

Hutt River Province

near Geraldton, WA 6530
AUSTRALIA
info@huttriver.net
www.huttriver.net

SMALL THINGS

Forget cavernous cathedrals and echoing abbeys, this tiny chapel is possibly the smallest place of worship in the world.

Frère Déodat came to Guernsey in 1913, and finding a little time on his hands he decided to construct a grotto. Inspired by this success he built a chapel two metres by three metres, but *quel dommage*, a visiting well-fed bishop could not get in the door, so he rebuilt, creating one double the size with a mosaic on the outside walls created from crushed crockery and stones sent to him from all over the world.

While we are on small things—whoever heard of leaping about over poor helpless babies? They've done it in Spain, though, for almost four centuries, and it is meant to bring health and safety (!) to these little ones.

Here's how it works: babies born in the previous year in Castrillo de Murcia are laid out on the pavement and their fathers dress up as devils and jump over them, cleansing them, or so they believe, of evil.

The Little Chapel

St Andrew
Guernsey
UK
Phone: +441481-72 35 52
(Tourist Office).
www.ghata.com

The Colacho—Baby Jumping Festival

Castrillo de Murcia

Burgos

SPAIN

john@johngordonross.com

http://spainforvisitors.com/sections/events_june.htm

When: Sunday following Corpus Christi

TESTING, TESTING

A brass plaque in the foyer of the Royal Oak Hotel, in Leominster, Herefordshire, announces that it is the 'spiritual home of the test card circle'. Test cards, as you are sure to want to know, are also called 'test patterns' and are the equivalent of a TV screensaver—providing something to look at until regular transmission resumes.

However, it seems that there is a growing number of people who find these patterns—and especially the background music that accompanies them—quite fascinating. So much so that several test card CDs have been released. More than that, every country differs in its perception of what the viewing (or the non-viewing) public would appreciate, and so you have the germ of an absorbing international hobby.

Test carders spend their spare moments collecting test cards and music from other countries, a sort of music-loving couch-potato version of train-spotting. New members are eagerly welcomed. Members enjoy the music, memorising where it is heard, and one glorious weekend a year, meet together at Leominster, near the Welsh border, to swap notes. Literally.

THE ROYAL OAK HOTEL
LEOMINSTER

SPIRITUAL HOME

of

THE TEST CARD CIRCLE

Founded in 1989 by
Paul Sawtell, Stuart Montgomery and Doug Bond

This plaque was unveiled on
6th April 2002 by St. John Howell,
writer and broadcaster

The Test Card Circle

175 Kingsknowe Road North
Edinburgh EH14 2DY UK
SCOTLAND
stuart.montgomery3@btopenworld.com
www.testcardcircle.org.uk

SIZE ISN'T EVERYTHING

Wales is generally regarded as a winner when it comes to the place with the longest name—Llanfairpwllgwyngyllgogerychwyrndrobwyll-llantysiliogogogoch—a jaw-breaking, breath-taking 60 letters.

But there is also the lesser-known New Zealand town with a Maori name: Taumatawhakatangihangakoauauotamateapokaiwhenuakitanatahu.

However, if you want one that is more a story than a title, try the Thai name for Bangkok which rhapsodises on about the city and beats everything else with 155 letters.

So how about the other end of the scale? Surprisingly, there are several towns with only *one* letter in their name.

Y, in Picardie, northwestern France, is pronounced 'ee' and its population is suspected to be about 30 Y-ites.

In the Arctic, Å, with a population of 150, is a tiny fishing village in the remote Lofoten Islands of northwest Norway.

Then there is Y, in the Matanuska-Susitna Borough of Alaska, considerably bigger, with a population of almost 60,000.

And just in case you were wondering—you were, weren't you?—there are three places in Scotland with only two letters in their name —Oa on the island of Islay, Ae, north of Dumfries, and Bu in Orkney.

TIME IN THE SUN

How about this? A 27-metre high sundial, accurate to within a minute. But wait, there's more. Jantar Mantar is one of the five observatories in India that were built in the 18th century. The Jaipur one, the largest, and with the most instruments, was built in 1728 to chart movements of the sun, moon and the known planets at the time, and to calculate eclipses.

This place could be mistaken for some surreal sculpture park, but look closer and you will find that each structure is actually a very specialised scientific instrument. It's just a very big stone one.

Like the huge sundial, accurate to twenty seconds, it has stairs in one tower so you can climb to the top for a better view of the park and the shadow falling on the exact time.

All this was the work of medieval astronomer Sawai Jai Singh, who was able to correct errors in the planetary tables of the day. If that's all a bit deep, just stand in awe that huge instruments built almost 300 years ago, without computers and using masonry tools, can be so accurate today.

Jantar Mantar Astronomy Park

Jaipur, Rajasthan
INDIA
Phone: +91 29430 90228
info@royalrajasthan.com
www.realrajasthan.com/jaipur-tourist.htm

TEMPTING...

Hillbilly fare has always been frugal and cost-cutting—but this is ridiculous! Not a drive-through takeaway. This is drive-*over* dining.

Or is it just a spoof? Turns out you don't get to eat *real* roadkill. The venison, frog, squirrel, and other varmints were not steam-rollered flat, visitors are told. Or were they?

Who knows—but they are all animals that have been eaten in the backwoods for many years, even though some may be new to visitors. So, fancy a nut-stuffed rattlesnake? Or hedgehog and cactus soup? Moose, anyone? Possum?

Entrants may saute or stir-fry, casserole or barbecue, but there's one simple rule: the main ingredients must be from animals or items that *could* be (and some old-timers may still use ones that have been) found on the road.

Some get carried away with the naming—'possum wrapped in tarmac' or even 'roadside ravioli' may feature on the menu.

But it's all in good stomach-turning fun.

Road Kill Cook-Off

Pocahontas County
Convention & Visitors Bureau
Marlinton, West Virginia
US
info@pocahontascountywv.com
www.pocahontas.org
When: late September

RIVER OF DREAMS

There are hotels and motels—and now Thailand has a floatel, established in 1976. But fear not, this raft doesn't float far. It is moored to the riverbank, so you won't wake up on a sandbank downstream, or even out to sea.

There's actually the best of both worlds here. On land, waterfalls, mysterious caves, and elephant rides over jungle trails—or simply the chance to dip in the river.

Kanchanaburi, 120 kilometres west of Bangkok, is the historical site of the bridge over the River Kwai, made memorable because it was built by Allied prisoners during the Japanese occupation. Nearby, there's also the Death Railway Train and a war museum that is not for the squeamish, and POW cemeteries, with thousands of graves.

Even reaching the raft by high-powered longtail boat is an adventure. And while the raft has no electricity, just kerosene lanterns and candles, it's a low-key back-to-nature experience, as all rooms have showers and toilets.

As well, there are two restaurant rafts, each seating 100 people and two theatrette rafts for the nightly folk dancing entertainment.

River Kwai Jungle Rafts & Floatel

THAILAND

info@riverkwaifloatel.com

www.riverkwaifloatel.com/index_jungle.htm

A DIVE-THROUGH POST OFFICE

There's never a postbox when you need one, is there? Vanuatu has noticed that problem and they're onto it, claiming to have set up the world's first Underwater Post Office.

To find it you need to dive off Hideaway Island on the outskirts of Vanuatu's capital, Port Vila. Located in three metres of water in a marine sanctuary surrounded by beds of coral and shoals of multicoloured fish and other marine life, this would have to be one of the world's most unusual, and possibly most beautiful, POs.

We know what you're thinking—and yes, the smart Vanuatans have come up with a special waterproof postcard that you can take on your swim to the letterbox. The egg-shaped fibreglass post office is staffed and your postcard is stamped by a postal worker, a certified diver, one of four who take shifts working underwater, and using a waterproof device. Can't dive? A staff member will zip down with it for you.

So how do you know when it's open for business? When the floating flag is up, of course.

Underwater Post Office

off Hideaway Island, Port Vila
VANUATU

tourism@vanuatu.com.vu

www.vanuatutourism.com

GO FOR A MOW

The slogan of the US Lawn Mower Racing Association is 'We turn a weekend chore into a competitive sport!' And in case you think this is another case of 'only in America', you need to know that there are associations all over the world that race lawnmowers. That's right! Just hop on your ride-on mower and off you go.

Across the Atlantic, in the UK, like many other slightly weird schemes this one began in the good old Cricketer's Arms in Wisborough Green, West Sussex. Deciding cars were too expensive, and motorised bar-stools and wheelbarrows not appropriate, the lads saw lawnmowers as the ideal economy vehicle.

In New Zealand, contestants fit little seats behind the lawnmowers, take the blades off them then race them around a paddock, although in Australia the sport seems fairly new, and yet to catch on properly.

But there is a European Cup and World Titles, so the sport is spreading. Just remember, you read about it here first.

US Lawn Mower Racing Association.

mowinfo@letsmow.com

www.letsmow.com

The British Lawn Mower Racing Association

info@blmra.co.uk

www.racemower.co.uk

DINING AT A HORSE'S PACE

In the 1890s this wooden bus, pulled by three Clydesdale draughthorses, may have been used to transport girls to their rather exclusive boarding school. Now it has been restored to become a horse-drawn restaurant complete with lace curtains and antique fittings. Three of Chris Wells' Clydesdale workhorses are harnessed up twice a day, ready and willing to take diners on a trip of a lifetime.

The appetiser is picked up opposite Australia's oldest pub, the Macquarie Arms, established in 1815, then it's a clip-clopping tour through the streets of Windsor in outer-Sydney, one of the area's oldest settlements, past waving bystanders.

The carriage is surprisingly roomy, allowing four couples to dine at a time, and the ride is so stable that even the wines are secure. With restaurant-standard food and wines, friendly and professional service, the whole meal and journey takes about four hours and is perhaps one of the most uniquely interesting ways to dine. A peep into Australia's past while enjoying today's fine food and wines.

Clydesdale's Restaurant

27 George Street
Windsor NSW 2756
AUSTRALIA
Phone: +612 4577 4544
www.clydesdalesrestaurant.com.au

BLIND TASTINGS

Just imagine not being able to see the food you're eating. Or your companion. But what if even the waiter was sight impaired? Torches, even luminous dials on watches are banned in these three places that operate in utter darkness. Why? So diners experience food without outside interference, but also to help understand the world of the blind.

Blind Cow began in 2001 to achieve understanding. Although diners are usually sighted, most staff—including chefs and bar staff—are visually impaired, wearing bells on their feet to let others know where they are. Other tricks include different-shaped plates for meat, vegetables and fish; drinks are weighed to prevent spills; and of course patrons need to call out to attract a waiter's attention.

Cologne's Unsicht-Bar has similar aims. Also opened in 2001, the popular restaurant's name translates as Blind Bar. And then there's 'Essen im Dunkeln', literally meaning 'eating in the dark', at the Conti Bistro in Germany, only on Friday and Saturdays every two weeks or so.

Could be the ideal venue for your next blind date!

Blind Cow Restaurant

Mill brook
Route 148 8008 Zurich
SWITZERLAND
Phone: +411 421 50 50
info@blindekuh.ch
www.blindekuh.ch/restaurant/restaurant.html

Unsicht-Bar

Gormannstr. 14
MI, Berlin
(Im Stavenhof 5–7 50668
Köln Cologne)
GERMANY
www.unsicht-bar.com

'Essen im Dunkeln'—Conti Bistro

Karlsplatz or Odeonsplatz
Munich
GERMANY
Phone: +498 93899 7784
info@essenimdunkeln.de
www.essenimdunkeln.de

IN THE ROCKS

Rather than having ice in your drinks, why not have your drinks in the ice? And in a departure from something that is becoming almost common in very cold countries, Auckland has pioneered an antipodean version.

Minus Five (which also happens to be the temperature) was created in 2004 from eighteen tonnes of ice, and everything—the seats, carvings, bar and cocktail glasses—are made of ice. It's cosy (if you can call an ice bar that) seating only 25, but you may stay for just 30 minutes, no doubt ordering New Zealand's own vodka—42 Below. But in this case the name refers to the latitude, not the temperature.

Minus Five

Princes Wharf
Auckland
NEW ZEALAND
Phone: +649 377 6702
tracey@fusionhospo.co.nz
www.minusfive.co.nz

Ice Bar

Nordic Sea Hotel

Vasagatan, Stockholm

SWEDEN

info@nordichotels.se

www.nordichotels.se/doc.open.asp?
DocID=54&StructID=2

Just 30 drinkers can snuggle into this chilly ice bar, opened in 2002. They are insulated from the −6°C temperature by lined silver cloaks, gloves and bootees which are given out at the door. Of course Absolut is absolutely the drink of choice.

Arctic Icebar

Yliopistokatu 5

Helsinki 00100

ICELAND

www.uniq.fi

And Helsinki's Uniq nightclub opens onto the minute Arctic Ice Bar made of ice from Lapland, and only large enough for twelve people muffled up in down coats and hoods.

SOME WATER WITH YOUR MEAL?

If you prefer fish to stay on your plate rather than swim past your table, this may not be the place for you. For here you are five metres under the surface, surrounded by 62 huge windows watching the sea creatures watching you—and every mouthful you take.

Not just a gimmick, this place is a 'green project' with front-row views of the marine park with showy reef fish and coral that environmentalists and divers have worked hard to protect.

Primarily this is a fun place to be surrounded by a constant reminder of the ocean, but rather than merely serving food and drink, the complex also offers a multi-media show and diver's school and club.

There are quirky aquatic features throughout the restaurant—which itself is starfish-shaped and designed by Israeli architect Josef Kiriaty.

Just for fun, the bar stools resemble jellyfish, and the bar displays a periscope from a submarine. Well, who knows? You might need it.

The Red Sea Star

The Southern Square
next to the Le Meridien Hotel
Eilat Bay
ISRAEL
Phone: +972-8-634-7777
gil@travelbyclick.com
www.inisrael.com/ipix/java/eilat_pub.htm

TRAM TREATS

Melbourne's trams are a city icon—but most people use them simply to get from one place to another. Dining in Melbourne is highly regarded too, and when you mix the two experiences, trams and dining, you're sure to get a real buzz.

The unique fleet of refurbished 1927 trams are really wine-red restaurants on wheels, and were the first travelling tramcar restaurants in the world. In 1983, the Colonial Tramcar Restaurants began rattling around the streets of Melbourne. Diners enjoy fine Australian wines and food and it is not hard to imagine what it must have been like a century ago when these vehicles were the fastest on the road.

Colonial Tramcar Restaurant

PO Box 372
Melbourne Victoria 3205
AUSTRALIA
Phone: +613 9696 4000
reservations@tramrestaurant.com.au
www.visitvictoria.com

The Tram-Restaurant

Carouge

Phone: +417 9321 3989

SWITZERLAND

tram@tele-restaurant.ch

www.tele-restaurant.ch/tramrestaurant/index_en.htm

In Carouge, Switzerland, wagons seating 58 diners, with a central kitchen between, move along with the city's normal traffic. The three-course meal takes about 90 minutes.

ALL AT SEA

The world's largest 'bathing pontoon' is moored 39 nautical miles off the Whitsunday coast. Reefworld's two floating platforms cater for up to 600 people, like a holiday camp in the middle of the ocean. There are talks by marine biologists too, so you can throw in some useful trivia to the next dinner party conversation, such as, 'Do you know where a starfish keeps its mouth?'

Snorkel, dive, swim, sunbake, or take a tour in the glass hulled semi-submersible coral viewer—better still, stay on overnight after the crowds go home. Called Reefsleep, guests can sleep-over (dinner and breakfast are included) and take their time to explore the reef, stargaze from the top deck, or descend to the underwater viewing chamber to get up close and personal with the weird and wacky-shaped reef fish and corals.

The catch is that this huge place only sleeps six people at any one time, so you will need to book well ahead.

Reefworld

11 Shute Harbour Road
Airlie Beach Qld 4802
AUSTRALIA
phone: +617 4946 5111
info@fantasea.com.au
www.fantasea.com.au

AND YOU THOUGHT IT WAS JUST FOR DRINKING!

Seems some people reckon that anything you can do above water, you can also do *in* it.

Like Underwater Ironing. These iron men and women (they're called ironists) take their unplugged iron and ironing board underwater and photograph each other. If you think this is weird, check out www.extremeironing.com for all the other places you can iron.

Then there's Underwater Hockey, played by two teams of six snorkellers on the bottom of a swimming pool. The stick is only about 30 centimetres long, and the puck is necessarily heavy, around 1.3 kilograms, so that it doesn't float off.

Underwater Rugby, another aquatic take on a land-based sport, is popular in Europe and the US. Each team has 15 players on a team, using snorkels in 3.5–5 metres depth of water. The ball is filled with salt water.

Extreme Underwater Ironing

webguy@diveoz.com.au
www.diveoz.com.au/aeui

Underwater Hockey

Phone: +151 0668 1621
kendallctv@aol.com
www.underwater-society.org

Underwater Rugby

KBurke@Haemonetics.com
www.underwater-society.org

TURKISH DELIGHTS

If watching grown men slip and slide over each other is your idea of a fun day out—read on. These slippery customers participate in what is said to be the oldest wrestling festival in the world. Kirkpinar oil wrestling began in 1357, in Rumelia, the European side of Turkey.

The events are meant to celebrate bravery—especially that of soldiers—as the festival stems from the time when the Ottomans entered the city. Apparently 40 wrestlers struggled to the death, providing the inspiration for these events that have persisted for almost 650 years.

The festivities and contests go on for a week with side attractions including feasting, folk dance and music, as any good festival does.

Oil Wrestling

Kirkpinar, Edirne
TURKEY
info@kirkpinar.com
www.kirkpinar.com
When: June

Camel Wrestling Championship

Selcuk
TURKEY
www.turkeycentral.com/Recreation_and_Sports/Camel_Wrestling/
When: January

Picture this: two testosterone-charged bull camels, and one female on heat. Remove the female and let the boys fight it out. It's not ugly. The camels lean on each other, push each other down, then finally the winner yells his victory.

YABBIE-DABBA-DOO

Cherax Destructor—that's the proper name for these mud-dwelling crustaceans that any Aussie country kid can wheedle out of a creek with his rotten-meat bait. However, in the last few decades they have begun to turn up on fine dinner plates in city restaurants and now many people make a livelihood from raising them. Others race them.

The small town of Talbot, under two hours from Melbourne, has a Yabbie Festival each Easter Saturday. You can fish for your yabbies in the middle of town, enter the races, and even qualify for the Yabbie Festival Corporate Cup if your steed is good enough. Of course there are cooked yabbies to try too.

Talbot Yabbie Festival

Phone: +613 5463 2555

Hotel Mulwala

86 Melbourne Street
Mulwala NSW 2647
AUSTRALIA
Phone: +613 5744 2245
When: Australia Day, 26 January

Kajabbi Yabby Races

Kajabbi Qld 4481
AUSTRALIA
Phone: +617 4742 5979
When: April

Windorah Yabby Races

Western Star Hotel
Windorah Qld 4481
AUSTRALIA
When: early September

BOGGED DOWN

No use pretending that bog snorkelling is an ancient Welsh custom that dates back to the Druids, one that sees the bog as a metaphor for adversity, and the winner as the saviour of the village. No, this relatively recent addition to the Welsh calendar of activities was purely commercial.

Llanwrtyd Wells, in Powys, Wales, is Britain's smallest town, and in 2001 the townsfolk decided they needed something to tempt visitors to the village. But all they had was a dense bog not far from town.

Bright idea time! Now, each August the bog bristles with snorkels, as eager entrants launch into the murky mud to bog snorkel. To qualify, racers must complete two lengths of a 55 metre bog trench. Fired up by the success of bog snorkelling, a new event has now been added—Mountain Bike Bog Snorkelling. For this—if you must know—the contestants have to cycle 90 metres through the bog.

And just when you thought it couldn't get any sillier, they have now added the Mountain Bike Bog Leaping Point To Point. Where will it end?

Bog Snorkelling

Waen Rhydd Peat Bog
Llanwrtyd Wells
WALES
(Postal Address: Ty Barcud,
Llanwrtyd, Powys LD5 4RB)
Phone: +441 5916 10666
http://llanwrtyd-wells.powys.org.uk/bog.htm
When: August Bank Holiday, a Monday

TWO FLIES CRAWLING UP A WALL

They say Aussies will bet on anything. We're betting you'll hardly believe these. The Story Bridge Hotel dates back to 1886, and it's here each January that a bucket of cockies is emptied in the middle of the 'race' ring. First one to the edge wins.

Cockroach Races

Story Bridge Hotel
Kangaroo Point Qld 4169
AUSTRALIA
Phone: +617 3391 2266
info@storybridgehotel.com.au
www.storybridgehotel.com.au/cockroachrace
When: Australia Day, 26 January

Cane Toad Races

Ironbar Bar & Restaurant
Macrossan Street
Port Douglas Qld 4871
AUSTRALIA
When: Tuesday and Thursday all year
also Maclean Cane Harvest Festival
Maclean NSW
AUSTRALIA
When: Late June
Cane toads are rather ugly amphibians, not much loved by Australians, but they do race well. Snails will compete if toads are not available, we're told.

Mt Compass Cow Races

Mt Compass SA 5210
AUSTRALIA
Phone: +618 8556 8393
When: Second Sunday in February
Dairy cows are ridden by 'jockey's', assisted by 'urgers' who help keep them mounted.

MORE FLIES

Huge interest in this event—and any sort of lizard can race. There was tragedy here, though, one year, as a plaque commemorates. A champion cockroach beat the champion lizard, but was killed soon afterwards when a drunk stood on it. *C'est la vie.*

Lizard Racing Championships

Paroo Track
Eulo Qld 4491
AUSTRALIA
Phone: +617 4655 2481
When: late-August/early-September

Dunny Derby

Winton Qld 4735
AUSTRALIA
Phone: +617 4657 1466
When: September every second year

In perhaps not the best of taste, but this is the outback after all. 'Dunny jockeys', enthroned in their outdoor loos on wheels, are towed by a partner.

Goanna Pulling Festival

Wooli Sportsground
Wooli NSW 2462
AUSTRALIA
Phone: +612 6649 7575
http://wooli.visitnsw.com
Easter Sunday

No, not a cruel and unusual sport. This entails a tug of war between two crouching men using heavy leather straps around their necks. Their stance makes them look like goannas. That's all.

Booligal Sheep Races

Booligal Cricket Ground
Booligal NSW 2711
AUSTRALIA
Phone: +612 6993 4045;
booligalsheepraces@hotmail.com
October long weekend

It's what it sounds like. A bunch of sheep racing. Still, it's a good excuse for a party and it draws the crowds to a small town that needs the visitors.

GET BOOKED

Antiquarians alert! Bookworms take notice! This town is your idea of heaven. Former market town Hay-on-Wye (35 kilometres from Hereford, and just over 250 kilometres from London) in the picture-postcard Wye Valley is really a book town, packed with an estimated one million books stacked on the shelves of its 30 bookshops. The trend began in 1961 when Richard Booth set up Boz Books, in Castle Street. This single bookshop turned into a string of shops, as he bought up whole libraries of books to stock them.

In one, a former cinema, Richard amassed 250,000 volumes, and the *Guinness Book of Records* named it the World's Largest Bookshop. Despite this, the place everyone talks about and photographs is the walled patch of grass at the foot of the Norman-built Hay Castle, lined with—yes, really—bookcases.

Here, weather permitting, you'll find 50 pence bargains in hard cover and paperback. Some people come to browse, others simply to sit on the wall and read, of course.

Hay-on-Wye

UK
Phone: +44 1497 821 771
www.hay-on-wye.co.uk

CAN DO

Beer is a vital fluid for Australians, and even the cans and cartons they come in achieve something of star status—particularly when they can be crafted into something really useful such as a craft that can be raced.

Mindil Beach is the venue for one of the last remaining Darwin icons—an annual race that has been repeated for around 30 years. It's pretty simple: build a raft, boat, or any other floatable creation from beer cans and be prepared to launch it and man it on the big day.

For added Aussie beach action there's thong throwing, and Henley on Mindil, for bottomless boats, as well as best hat and clothing contests with the same rules—gear must be made from old cans, boxes or cartons.

Beer Can Regatta

Darwin NT
AUSTRALIA
Phone: 0411 560 619
beercanregatta@hotmail.com.
When: mid-August

And whoever thought you needed water for a regatta? The rarely flowing Todd River, 1500 kilometres from any large body of water, hosts a hugely popular annual boat race. The dry riverbed is used for a Red Centre version of 'eights', 'Oxford tubs'—even bathtubs—and yacht races, as well as landlubber events, with all proceeds going to charity.

Henley on Todd Regatta

Alice Springs NT 0871
AUSTRALIA
phone: +618 8952 3040
www.henleyontodd.com.au
When: 3rd Saturday
in September

JUMBO GYRATIONS

Playing polo seated on an elephant rather than a horse seems about as awkward as playing football on stilts. Yet this amazing 'take' on the upper-class horsey-crowd English sport was popular over a century ago in India—devised, of course, by the British—then, using a soccer ball.

The pitch is shorter, as elephants are not as fast, nor turn as quickly, but the rules are similar to those for horseback polo, although each player has a mahout (trainer) on board to direct the elephant.

The World Elephant Polo Association was formed in 1982, with games now conducted using a standard polo ball, and two or three metre bamboo stick fitted with a standard polo mallet. The annual contest attracts players from many countries.

Elephant Polo

Tiger Tops Lodge
Royal Chitwan National Park
NEPAL
info@elephantpolo.com
www.elephantpolo.com
When: December

In Thailand, due to deforestation, elephants are no longer needed for logging work. To preserve the elephants—and also the rare endangered ones—the Lampang Elephant Conservation Centre encourages unemployed jumbos to turn to culture, by playing musical instruments—and painting.

The elephants hold a paintbrush in their trunks and create bold sweeping artworks, much in demand by Impressionist art lovers.

Elephant Artists

28–29 Lampang-Chiangmai Road
Lampang
THAILAND
Phone: +66 5422 8108, +66 5422 8034
elephant@fio.or.th
www.elephant.com/catalog/thailand.php

Weird and Wacky · 181

CAMEL CULTURE

Camels were brought to Australia in the 1800s by Afghan cameleers and were used extensively in outback Australia, where many still roam wild. These giant beasts don't look as if they are built for speed, but today they make exciting steeds in a variety of inland camel races in Queensland and the Northern Territory.

The Bedourie Camel Cup is almost 1000 kilometres inland from Brisbane and attracts many people to the camel racing providing entertainment for the whole family.

Bedourie Camel Cup

Bedourie Race Track
Keplar Street
Bedourie Qld 4829
AUSTRALIA
Phone: +617 4746 1277
When: mid-July

Based on professional camel races run in the United Arab Emirates, races here cover between three–ten kilometres. This racing program takes the business very seriously, while still proving a fun day out, beginning the night before with a wild camel catching contest.

Boulia Camel Races

Boulia Showgrounds
Boulia Qld 4829
AUSTRALIA
Phone: +617 4746 3144
Fax: +617 4746 3191
www.queenslandholidays.com
/outback/525915/index.cfm

CAMEL-LOT

Alice Springs is almost exactly in the middle of Australia. No wonder they call this area the Red Centre. And no wonder camels do well here, as the red sand is perfect for them.

So it stands to reason that the annual Camel Cup—begun in 1970 as a bet, as all good ideas seem to be in Australia—is a hit. Ships of the desert they may be, but here they turn into racing steeds down the dry Todd riverbed.

Appropriately run at Blatherskite Park, the cup has developed into a huge attraction with wacky races. The Honeymoon Handicap has 'grooms' beginning the race and a takeover midway by 'brides' that hop on the kneeling beast and race to the finish line.

Camel Cup

PO Box 3233
Alice Springs NT 0871
AUSTRALIA
Phone: +618 8952 3040
info@camelcup.com.au.
www.camelcup.com.au
When: mid-July

For a mix of creatures, though, head for Charleville in Queensland's outback. Camel races are usually jockeyed by seasoned riders, but the donkey races—should you read something into that name?—are open to all those game enough to try. Yabbie races are left to the yabbies. They hasten to the edge of the piece of canvas, while the temporary 'owners' make bets and cheer them on.

Charleville Camel, Donkey & Yabbie Race Festival
Charleville Qld
AUSTRALIA
Phone: +617 4654 2102
When: first week in August

MY FESTIVAL WON'T COME BACK

You would expect that Australia would host the World Boomerang Championships every year, wouldn't you? But not so. Contestants for the World Boomerang Cup have gathered in many countries, recently Germany and France, and the surprise is that there are so many teams involved. There are strict rules and the contest is judged on both team and individual accuracy.

The boomerang is an indigenous Australian throwing lure, used in hunting to tease birds into believing it is a bird of prey. And you may not believe it, but many boomerangs are not designed to return.

Boomerangs are shaped similarly to aircraft wings, giving them lift and distance. And a collection of sticks very similar to boomerangs was also found in King Tut's tomb in Egypt.

The first Boomerang World Cup was held in Australia in 1988, but now competition boomerangs are made from tough Finnish birch and teams from all over the world compete.

Makes you wonder when the competition will return to Australia.

World Boomerang Championships

Charleville-Mézière
FRANCE
http://wbc.boomerangs.net
When: mid-July

CROSS PURPOSES

These small hills at Siauliai, northwest of Vilnius, Lithuania's capital, are eerie and arresting. They have been the site of crosses for many years, although no-one knows for sure who started erecting them. The city of Siauliai (pronounced shoe-lay) dates from 1236, and it seems placing crosses in a prominent position has always been the Lithuanian way of showing resistance to foreign oppressors, beginning in the 14th century when the country was occupied by Teutonic knights.

It is said that before 1991, while the Soviet Union was in power in Lithuania, authorities cleared the hillocks with bulldozers three times, but within weeks the crosses had returned, sprouting again as if by divine intent.

Huge crosses support smaller crosses, tiny plastic ones swing from slightly larger ones, a multitude of them, and then there are rosaries, holy pictures, badges and medals as well, a tribute to Christianity and national identity. Pope John Paul II even visited the Hill of Crosses, in September 1993.

Attempts have been made to count the crosses, but all failed. One person counted a million, then gave up, still far short of the total. Unique and haunting, still they hang, rattling in the wind, the number accumulating daily.

SPA-OUT!

Imagine receiving a massage in the branches of a banyan tree! At Bora Bora Lagoon Resort there are six treatment rooms, a list of Tahitian treatments, and a menu of centuries-old remedies based on South Pacific herbs and spices—what more could you want? Maybe some help getting back to earth after such a heavenly experience.

Or go underwater for your therapy at the Huvafen Fushi spa in the Maldives. The spa is based around the benefits of the seas, so why not go one step more and build the world's first underwater therapy rooms? Now you can bliss out in the waterproof underwater spa with the fish all around.

Perhaps it's not so new. In ancient Roman times people bathed in curative waters, now you can be pummelled while the Indian Ocean and its creatures flow all around you. It puts a whole new spin on 'hydrotherapy'.

Huvafen Fushi

North Male Atoll
MALDIVES
info@huvafenfushi.com
www.huvafenfushi.com

Treetop Spa

Bora Bora Lagoon Resort
Motu Toopua, BP 175—98730

Vaitape, Bora Bora,
FRENCH POLYNESIA

apoole@orientx.net

www.boraboralagoon.com

CAFE BIZARRE

This comes from the fertile imagination of the man who has sited one hotel in a tree in a park and another in a lake with sleeping quarters underwater. Genberg's buildings-cum-art installations are never going to be staid, so how would you expect him to design a café, society's premier place of relaxation?

With the strangely antipodean name, Café Koala, and Genberg as the creator, you have to expect some surprises. Certainly, you'll need a steady hand to ascend the ladder with your cappuccino to one of the eight five-metre high chairs placed in a circle. Best to go up there with a bunch of friends, perhaps. 'A slightly new angle to the coffee experience,' their creator calls it. 'Seeking relaxation by tension.'

The idea is that you conquer your fears, relax, sit back with your mates—also intrepid, one would suppose—and look down on those who haven't made it yet. Oh, and enjoy your coffee at the same time.

You can bet the other residents in Genberg's home town of Vasteras may be wondering what he will come up with next!

Café Koala

Vasteras
SWEDEN
mikael@konst.org
genberg@beta.telenordia.se
www.konst.org/genberg/engtext.htm

LOOK, MUM, NO BUNGEE!

If you thought bungee jumping was a modern fad, then check out the Pentecost Islanders who have been doing it for many years.

The traditional land-diving ceremony is held on Saturdays throughout April and May, but there are no high-tech cords for these guys. Instead, they use supple liana vines, more elastic after the wet season, and attached to 20–30 metre high tree towers.

Nor is it a show-off event. This fertility rite is gender specific for guys only, and some as young as seven years old take part.

The story goes that long ago an angry husband chased his wife to the top of a tree. She jumped. He followed. But she had secured a vine to her ankles. Never more, say male Vanuatans, will a woman trick them.

So, after the yam harvest has begun each year, the men set up the towers. But, just like packing your own chute, each diver must select his own vine. This is critical, as the aim is for just a land-diver's shoulders to touch the ground, and there have been times when the length has been misjudged, with tragic results.

Land Diving

VANUATU

P&O Cruises (www.pocruises.com.au) have cruises to Pentecost Island

www.vanuatutourism.com

Phone: 132 469 (in Australia)

When: Saturdays, April and May

A COMMUNITY GETS ARTISTIC

Wellington, in New South Wales, is not quite outback, but it's on the way. And located just a few kilometres south of the town is a very strange contemporary sculpture that has become a bit of a landmark.

Like most modern art, it needs to be explained. And the spiel goes something like this: The arch—also seen as the gateway to the region—is thin and skeletal, representing the many fossils discovered in the vicinity of the nearby Wellington Caves, while the wind chimes resemble stalactites.

The dome, the creators say, is meant to suggest the magnificent sunsets in the area, and the seedpod shape of the structures and the plants relate to the fertility of the lush Macquarie Valley. A pool represents the waters of the Bell and Macquarie rivers which mingle here, while the wall and totem shapes give homage to the Catombal Range in the background.

The mosaic work was carried out by locals and school groups and is a fascinating blend of present events and local history. In fact the foundation of the main structure and the wall were girders of the old Wellington Bridge which collapsed in 1989, when an overweight truck attempted to cross it.

Wellington Gateway

cnr Mitchell Highway
& Wellington Caves Rd
Wellington NSW
AUSTRALIA
(Wellington Tourist Centre
Nanima Crescent
Wellington NSW 2820)
Phone: +612 6845 1733,
1800 621 614

COLD COMFORT

It's not exactly the place to nip out to for a swift pint, but this is about as far south as it gets if you are looking for a cold one.

Vernadsky (formerly Faraday) Research Station on Galindez Island in the Argentine Islands Archipelago, established in 1947, is the oldest operational station in the Antarctic Peninsula, and is located 65.15°S.

Here snow falls on around 250 days a year and summer temperatures range between freezing and 2°C. In winter it's much colder, plummeting to −25°C, but then no-one visits the twenty or so Russian scientists who work here studying the weather and the hole in the ozone layer.

In fact, only a few people even come in summer, and they arrive in Zodiacs launched from cruise ships to the area. If you do make it here, however, you can buy a drink in the world's most southern bar.

There is also a tiny gift shop and a place to mail your postcard—though don't hold your breath. Depending on the arrival of ships to take away the mailbags, it may not be delivered for up to nine months!

With penguins and seals the main company here, visitors are welcome. And you can be sure there is no shortage of ice for your drinks.

Peregrine Adventures

258 Lonsdale Street
Melbourne Victoria 3000
AUSTRALIA
Phone: +613 9663 8611
websales@peregrine.net.au
www.peregrine.net.au/
antarctica/index.asp

LIQUID ASSETS

Some countries use their canals and rivers like roads, so why not sell from them as well?

Deep in Vietnam's 'rice bowl', at Can Tho, on the Mekong River, every morning is market day at the Cai Rang Floating Market. Hundreds of craft jostle on the muddy waters and each has their sale sign out and is loaded with all sorts of tropical fruit and vegetables, fish and packs of rice-paper sheets. You can tell what's for sale by the food hanging from the tall pole above the boat, so when something is sold out, the 'sign' is simply removed.

In Thailand, the Damnoen Saduak Floating Market is located at Damnoen Saduak District, Ratchaburi Province. Here traders ply the 32-kilometre canal, dug in the mid-1860s to connect the Mae Klong River with the Tacheen River.

The rich soil is ideal for growing all sorts of fruit and vegetables and the locals set up their water-based shops each day. In Bangkok, noisy longtail boats will ferry passengers through markets offering souvenirs to tourists.

Shopping is easy. Make your choice, then just go with the flow.

www.vietnamtourism.com/e_pages/vietnam/ province/infor/cantho.htm

www.bangkoksite.com/Ratchaburi/FloatingMarket/FloatingMarket1.htm

OCTOPUSSY ISLAND

Funny thing about the movies. They can take a well-known and beautiful place and make it even more famous. Like the Lake Palace, built on an island in the middle of a gorgeous lake in Udaipur in northwestern India. That should stake its claim to fame, surely? Yet mention it, and most people will reply. 'Oh, that's where a Bond movie was filmed, wasn't it?'

Originally built on an island in Lake Pichola in the 17th century as a royal summer retreat, the white marble palace is a low-key take on some of Shah Jahan's buildings at Agra. You know—the famous ones. Today it's an ultra-smart hotel, and the idea of 007 swanning around in the lake seems a trifle incongruous.

However, this was not the only place in town used for filming *Octopussy*. The Monsoon Palace on a hill high above the city was the villain's hideout, and many scenes were shot in other parts of the city. It is even said that there is a café somewhere in the city that plays the film non-stop.

Lake Palace Hotel

Udaipur, Rajasthan
INDIA
info@lake-palace-udaipur.com
www.tajhotels.com

FOLLY GOOD

Helga (De Silva) Blow could never be accused of being dull. Nor would her house, which she whimsically calls her 'folly'. In fact the whole place is vibrant and brimming with colour, a mix of old and new furniture in strange shapes and interesting combinations.

Born into one of Sri Lanka's premier political dynasties—Helga's father was at one time the Sri Lankan Ambassador in Paris—since 1993 she has been busy creating an Art Deco hotel in what was once her family home.

Now this 1930s building (once a 'rather grim hotel' in the 1960s) is lush with walls covered with newspaper clippings and art, stag heads, weapons, mirrors, and Gothic bits and bobs.

The 40 guestrooms with their fabulous views follow many themes: jungle and tropical, crazily flamboyant, or simply wacky. With arty eccentricity, sort of Picasso meets the Addams family, there's a sunny warmth too.

Helga wouldn't have it any other way. And nor would most of her gobsmacked guests, you suspect.

Helga's Folly

32 Frederick E de Silva
Mawatha
Kandy
SRI LANKA
Phone: +94 81 223 4571
Fax: +94 81 447 9370
enquiries@helgasfolly.com
www.helgasfolly.com

BRUSHES WITH FAME

Tito slept here. In fact, this summerhouse once hosted anyone who was anybody in Europe and beyond. First belonging to Tito, president of Slovenia, Vila Bled is now a prestigious hotel, originally constructed from the same shimmering marble as another President's home thousands of kilometres away—the White House in Washington, DC.

Haile Selassie, King Hussein, Nikita Khrushchev, Jawaharial Nehru, Indira Gandhi and Gamal Nasser all stayed here, and they certainly would have been wowed with the fabulous postcard-perfect view of Lake Bled and its island church and the 1000-year-old fortress perched on the cliff beyond.

In the 18th century the castle's owner saw the lake as a potential clay-pit and tossed around the idea of draining away the waters. Luckily he didn't, as the 9th-century lake church is a favourite of tourists (including wedding parties) who get there by using hand-propelled gondolas.

On nearby farms watch out for the world's most beautiful beehives. It's a custom here to paint cute and colourful folktale images on them.

Hotel Vila Bled

Cesta svobode 26
SI-4260 Bled
SLOVENIA
Phone: +386 4579 1500
hotel@vila-bled.com
www.vila-bled.com/en-contact.html

Picture credits:

Page. 7, Helen Russ; pp. 9, 45, 59, 113, 139, Sally Hammond; p. 13, Mark Hatter; pp. 15, 17, 21, 55, 69, 73, 85, 97, 137, 141, 143, 153, 187, 189, Gordon Hammond; p. 19, Gajudju Crocodile Holiday Inn; p. 23, Steven Williams; p. 25, David and Julie Hinds; p. 27, courtesy of King Pacific Lodge; p. 29, courtesy Ottowa Jail Hostel; p. 33, 99, David Greenberg; p. 35, courtesy of Nubian Nile Cruises; p. 37, courtesy Mrs Lou Rapley; p. 41, Tony Wheeler; p. 51, Peter and Priscilla Roberts; p. 57, International Tourism Club; p. 63, Used with permission of Capsule Hotels; p. 67, Ice Palace Inn; p. 73, courtesy of Werribee Zoo Park; p. 77, David McGonigal; p. 79, Gordon Ward; p. 81, courtesy Landmark Trust UK; p. 83, courtesy of Old Gaol Backpackers; p. 93, Suha Ersoz; p. 95, courtesy of Kokopelli's Cave; p. 101, courtesy of East Brother Light Station; pp. 102–103, Ev an Stein and Duyen Nguyen; p. 105, courtesy Bill Lam; p. 107, Tapio Tikka; p. 115, courtesy of KNTO; p. 117, Brian Hammond; p. 121, Tourism Authority of Thailand; p. 122, courtesy Shetland Islands Tourism; p. 125, Used with permission Shane Pym; p. 133, courtesy Turkish Culture and Tourism Office; p. 145, Nancy McComb Smithson; p. 149, David Ellis; p. 156, courtesy of Minus 5 Ice Bar; pp. 158–159, Israel Ministry of Tourism; p. 161, courtesy Tourism Victoria; p. 172, courtesy Tourism Queensland; p. 174, Peter Lik, courtesy of Queensland Tourism; p. 179, Bae Hooper; p. 181, Catherine Ryan, Novica; pp. 183, 184, 185, Bae Hooper; p. 191, used with permission of Huvafen Fushi Treetop Spa.